THE HEART OF CHRISTIANITY

GW00694571

THE HEART OF CHRISTIANITY

ROMANS 1-8 / GRAEME RUTHERFORD

AN ALBATROSS BOOK

the bible reading fellowship
OPENING THE BIBLE

© Commentary: Graeme Rutherford 1991
© Discussion questions: Albatross Books Pty Ltd 1991

Published in Australia and New Zealand by
Albatross Books Pty Ltd
PO Box 320, Sutherland
NSW 2232, Australia
in the United States of America by
Albatross Books
PO Box 131, Claremont
CA 91711, USA
and in the United Kingdom by
The Bible Reading Fellowship
Peter's Way, Sandy Lane West
Oxford OX4 5HG, England

First edition 1991
Second edition 1993

This book is copyright. Apart from any fair dealing for the purposes of private study, research, criticism or review as permitted under the Copyright Act, no part of this book may be reproduced by any process without the written permission of the publisher.

National Library of Australia
Cataloguing-in-Publication data

Rutherford, Graeme
The Heart of Christianity

ISBN 0 86760 096 9 (Albatross)
ISBN 0 7459 2810 2 (BRF)

1. Bible. N.T. Romans — Study I. Title

227.106

Cover photo: John Graham
Printed and bound in Australia by McPherson's Printing Group, Victoria

Contents

Dedication

**To the memory of my mother,
killed in a car accident 22 June 1989**

Whenever I read Romans, God teaches me afresh that Murphy's Law still operates, but that trustful acceptance of life as it comes, and keeping on doing what I should, are the two keys to happiness both here and hereafter.

Acknowledgements

The author gratefully acknowledges the help given on the *Bibliography* by Dr Robert Banks, Professor of the Ministry to the Laity, Fuller Theological Seminary, California, USA and Dr James D.G. Dunn, Professor of Theology, University of Durham, UK.

Unless otherwise indicated, all Bible references are from the *New Revised Standard Version*, © copyright 1989, Division of Christian Education of the National Council of the Churches of Christ in the United States of America.

Introduction

GENTLE PRODDING, PERSUASION, cajoling and even bribery have been used by me to ensure that my five children learn slabs of Romans by heart. They do not always appreciate it — though most of the time we make it a fun family activity. I think that there is no better foundation for their future than a clear grasp of this important letter. Strange as it may seem, knowing Romans by rote helps to get the meaning clearer.

Our family is not alone in delighting in this book. For many theologians in the early church, the letter to the Romans represented the high peak of scripture. Likewise the sixteenth century Reformers felt that they were at the summit of an Alpine ascent when they reached this New Testament letter.

Martin Luther referred to it as 'the clearest Gospel of all'[1] and John Calvin claimed that 'if a man understands it, he has a sure road opened for him to the understanding of the whole scripture.[2]

The contemporary Australian monk Michael Casey, of Tarrawarra Abbey on the outskirts of Melbourne, claims that the decline of individuals and societies is due to heedlessness of God causing the degradation described in the first chapter of Romans.

But the message of Romans is not limited to monks or theologians. As the scholar Paul Achtemeier says, while the letter is 'unashamedly theological in its approach. . . Paul meant his letter to be read or heard and understood by "lay" men and women in the church in Rome. It is intended as a letter for practising Christians.'[3]

It is good news for all people and there is no telling what may happen when its words hit home. It is fair to say that all roads in the Bible lead to Romans and the rest of the Bible is seen most clearly from this letter. As we seek to understand the message of this book, we will often be surprised at how Paul packs a lot into a very short space. But there are some key principles to keep in mind as we read this tightly written book that will help us understand its meaning for us today.

1. Romans requires hard thinking

The letters to the Corinthians, Galatians and Thessalonians have a distinctly personal character: each seems directed to a specific situation in the church which Paul knew intimately. Romans, on the other hand, was written as a means of Paul introducing himself to a church he had not visited and of clearly setting out a comprehensive and reasoned statement of the fundamentals of Christianity. It is therefore more philosophical than the other books. It reveals that Paul — divinely inspired (as I believe he was) or not — was a man of considerable intellect and logical reasoning, to be ranked with such profound thinkers as Origen, Chrysostom, Augustine of Hippo, Thomas Aquinas, Martin Luther, John Calvin and Karl Barth.

Paul's letter is marvellous, mind-stretching theology, an excellent antidote to 'mindless Christianity'. Now admittedly such theological reflection does not turn some people 'on'. Many Christians, in the words of Michael Harper, 'have so convinced themselves that they cannot think themselves *into* blessing, they are fearful that they will think themselves *out of* blessing. What is needed is a little less hot air, and many more cool breezes of the Spirit to chill the brain, clear away the mists of mindless uncertainties and get what Agatha Christie's little Belgian detective, Hercule Poirot, always used to call "the little grey cells" to work properly.'[4]

The reader of Romans is required to think strenuously and follow carefully Paul's reasoned argument. A great deal can be packed into a tiny word. For example, we must pay close attention to the *conjunctions* which link the sentences in logical steps. Here is a case in point.

In the theme sentence of the letter, Paul's connecting words introduce the grounds on which his previous statements are based:

Romans 1, verses 16-18
16. '*For* I am not ashamed of the gospel, because it is the power of God for the salvation of everyone who believes: first for the Jew, then for the Gentile.
17. *For* in the gospel a righteousness from God is revealed. . .
18. *For* the wrath of God is being revealed. . .'

The New International Version of the Bible inconveniently omits the conjunction 'for' at the beginning of verses 16 and 18. Careful attention to Paul's connecting words forces the reader to observe the relationship of the various parts of a sentence to each other. If we could engage the apostle in conversation, the sequence of his argument in the above verses might be expanded and set out as follows:

Question: Paul, you say you are eager to preach the gospel in Rome. What lies at the root of your eagerness to share the good news?
Answer: Well, others in the imperial capital may be tempted to be ashamed of a message about a crucified carpenter, but I am far from being ashamed of it. This message is invested with the power of God which results in salvation for all

who believe.
Question: How is this?
Answer: Because in the gospel it is revealed that people get a right standing from God. This right standing can be theirs by faith.
Question: And why is this necessary, Paul?
Answer: Well, because the wrath of God is being revealed from heaven against all the godlessness and wickedness. . .

In verses 16, 17 and 18 the conjunction 'for' links what follows with what precedes and amplifies the previous statement.

In its use of such connections, Romans stands in contrast to the four Gospels. The Gospel authors — and Mark in particular — loosely connect the various incidents in Jesus' life and ministry with connecting words such as 'and' or 'immediately'. There is no necessary connection between what goes before and what follows. Romans is different. Everything is 'because', 'for', 'since' and 'so' — logical steps from one point to the next. Paul is a vigorous thinker, with a profound respect for logic and disciplined argument.

As well as paying close attention to the elements of Paul's tightly-packed argument, we need to keep in mind the overall theological *structure* of the book. Like many of Paul's letters, there are two main sections:

Part A: a *doctrinal* section (chapters 1 to 11)
Part B: an *ethical* section (chapters 12 to 16)

We are studying only chapters 1 to 8. For this section, the key to the overall structure is to be found in the quotation from Habakkuk in chapter 1, verse 17. This can be translated as: 'The righteous-by-faith shall live.' Romans 1, verse 18 to chapter 4, verse 25 is an exposition of what it means to be righteous-by-faith. Chapters 5, 6, 7 and 8 explain what it really means 'to live'.

This letter was written by Paul probably in late AD 55/early 56, or late 56/early 57. The fact that we have such a developed theology so early runs counter to the fashionable idea that there was a tidy progression of thought from the early Christians through Paul's writings to the crowning theological summit of John's Gospel.

No-one denies that there is development, but it could not have been development in a straight line. Romans with its profound theology stands too near the beginning of New Testament literature to allow us to plot neatly the advance of New Testament doctrine. In any case, development is rarely as simple as some ivory-tower academics assume.

As Dr Leon Morris astutely observes, 'One thinker makes great advances, but the next in line is as likely to go back as to go forward. . . Genius is not the result of building painstakingly on the work of predecessors.'[5]

2. Romans places a precondition on us

New Testament writer C.E.B. Cranfield pays tribute to John Calvin in these words:

> If we had to choose just one word to characterise Calvin's commentary on Romans, it would be the word 'humble', for it seems to us to display to an outstanding degree that humility before the text which is shared to some degree by every commentator on a historical document who is of any worth — the humility which seeks, not to master and manipulate, but to understand and to elucidate.[6]

We may not like what we read in Romans. It may make us very angry and frustrated. Paul sets forward in this book the terms of admittance into God's heaven. We must humbly acknowledge it is God's heaven and that he has the prerogative to set the terms of entry.

Leon Morris uses a homely illustration:

> If I go along to a football match and discover that the charge for admittance is, say [here we must update], fifteen dollars, I may object furiously. I may say to the man at the gate, 'I know both these teams. Neither of them is capable of a good performance. They could not possibly put on a game which would be worth fifteen dollars to see. I'll pay *eight*!' But no matter how

> firmly I hold this point of view, I cannot impose it on the gatekeeper. If I argue with him along these lines, he will have nothing to do with me. In fact, there are only two courses open to me. I can pay the fifteen dollars and go in and see the match or I can keep my money and stay out. What I cannot do is to fix an admittance charge that satisfies me, pay that and go in. It is not my right to fix the admittance charge. I can take it or leave it. But I cannot modify it.[7]

A similar situation holds in the spiritual realm. We can enter heaven on God's terms or we can stay out. That may sound abrasive, but it is in fact the path of humility. We must allow God to be God. We cannot impose our will on him by changing what we do not like in scripture.

Our minds need to be engaged as we wrestle with the meaning of Romans. We must not stifle our intellect, but we must humble it and resist the temptation to rewrite Paul.

3. Romans centres on God, not doctrinal disputes

During the stormy period of the Reformation, the message of 'justification by grace alone through faith alone' became the touchstone of orthodoxy. It was supported by frequent reference to Romans. In these conflicts it was all too easy by the process called 'projection' to think of the legalists against whom

Paul battled as 'Catholics' and those who had grasped Paul's message as 'Lutherans'. In other words, the Protestant-Catholic debate was too easily read back into the New Testament.

To say this is in no way to suggest that the doctrine of 'justification by grace alone through faith alone' is not central to Romans. It is. But even this important doctrine is not seen for what it is if it is not seen from Paul's perspective.

Paul sets all that he has to say in Romans in a *God-centred* framework. Leon Morris has conducted a word-count analysis on this letter and produced some fascinating results. He has shown, for example, that after the definite article 'the' and the words 'and' and 'in', the word most frequently used is 'God':

> Paul's treatment of themes like justification or sanctification or predestination have so caught the imagination of scholars and others that they have tended to concentrate on them and to overlook the dominance of the God-theme. . . Romans is a book about God and we must bear the fact in mind in all our interpretation of what it says. Otherwise, we shall miss some of the wonderful things it says.[8]

It was this theocentric perspective which, according to the English theologian P.S. Watson in his book *Let God be God*, was responsible for the revolution in Martin Luther's life.

In religion it is possible, even where we *claim* to be theocentric, to think of ourselves as the centre around which all else, including God, moves. We seek God in pursuit of our *own* interests. In yearning for present peace of heart and mind, we seek God no less for our own satisfaction than if we sought material advantages at his hands.

In the gospel — as Luther understood it — the question of our relationship with God does not lie finally with ourselves. He is not moved by our merits. On the contrary, we are moved by him. Luther had penetrated the theme of Romans better than many of his successors — that of God being central. It is a dominant theme which can yet be overlooked by reading Romans through the polemical grid of later centuries.

God, then, is the orbit around which we revolve. The subject of Romans, according to Paul Achtemeier, is 'the relationship of creation to its Creator and Lord'. He goes on to say that Paul's conviction in Romans is that 'the only way a creature can survive is if that creature enjoys the continuing favour of the Creator.'[9]

4. Paul is limited by language restrictions

No-one has made this clearer than Professor C.E.B. Cranfield in his studies on Paul's attitude to the law. His researches have shown that the Greek language of Paul's day possessed no word-group corresponding to our terms like 'legalism', 'legalist' and 'legalistic':

> This means that [Paul] lacked a convenient terminology for expressing a vital distinction, and so was surely seriously hampered in the work of clarifying the Christian position with regard to the law. In view of this, we should always. . . be ready to reckon with the possibility that Pauline statements, which at first sight seem to disparage the law, were really directed not against the law itself, but against that misunderstanding and misuse of it for which we now have a convenient terminology. In this very difficult terrain Paul was pioneering.[10]

So, for example, when Paul says in chapter 6, verse 14, 'you are not under law, but under grace', he is using a shorthand form of writing which may mean:

> you are not under law's condemnation, but
> under grace God's favour, *OR*
> you are not under the perversion of the law,
> which is legalism, but under grace.

Paul's attitude to the law is a thorny area of modern exegesis. We will say more about that when we come to consider chapter 7. But it is important at the outset to appreciate Paul's difficulty in trying to say something for which there were no convenient terms at hand. He was breaking new ground — not only in evangelism or theology, but in language itself.

Not everyone accepts C.E.B. Cranfield's thinking. Stephen Westerholm challenges Cranfield's 'shorthand' theory. He writes:

> Whether or not the Greek language possessed a suitable single word for 'legalism', it surely provided — and Paul's vocabulary included — sufficient resources for indicating whether he was speaking of the law as intended by God or in the (allegedly) perverted form in which it was regarded by Jews.[11]

There is also the so-called 'new perspective on Paul' which does not see the problem with which Paul contends as one of legalism at all. Theologian Professor James Dunn claims that this 'meritorious approach' to law was based in part 'on the Reformation rejection of a system where indulgences could be bought and merits accumulated'. He agrees that the Reformation protest was necessary, but warns against an *illegitimate transfer* of sixteenth-century presuppositions to the first century.

According to James Dunn, the Judaism of the first century was based on the premise of grace — that God had freely chosen Israel and made his covenant with Israel. This covenant relationship was regulated by law — not as a way of entering the covenant or of gaining merit, but as a way of living *within* the covenant. Such a view of law has been styled 'covenantal nomism'.

Dunn and other scholars are right when they warn us against 'an illegitimate transfer of later ideas and presuppositions to the first century'. It is always a danger but, as already pointed out, it is *also* illegitimate to transfer meaning from the background of the New Testament writers to the foreground.

The idea of grace can certainly be found among some of the Jews of Paul's time, but so can the 'treasury merit' approach to law. Certainly Jesus' parable of the Pharisee and tax collector makes it clear that the notion of earning salvation by the merit of good works was not unknown in the first century. Faith itself was often understood by the Jews as a *meritorious work*.

Thus we read: 'The faith which your father Abraham believed in me [God] merits that I should divide the sea. . .'

Or again: 'Our father Abraham became the heir of this and the coming world simply by the merit of the faith with which he believed in the Lord. . .' (Mekilta Exodus 14: 15 and 31).

The 'new perspective' on Paul exaggerates the case by eliminating from among Paul's opponents those who were teaching a system of earning salvation by merit. Cranfield's suggestion of taking the phrase 'not under law' as shorthand for 'not under legalism' is one possible explanation and, in spite of recent interpreters, it makes good sense from what we know of Paul's opponents.

5. Romans speaks to the twentieth century, but needs 'translating'

Much of the fatigue of modern living comes from the fact that people are driven along by an almost obsessive need for self-justification. Paul's letter to the Romans, with its liberating message of justification, speaks with power and relevance to this modern predicament. It goes to the root of the modern society's *angst* problem.

As Australian theologian Robert Banks perceptively comments:

> At the root of our busyness and haste lies either a flight *from* ourselves, others and God, or a desire to justify ourselves *to* God, others and ourselves. In other words, our activism is either idolatrous self-absorption or a self-justifying exercise. In whole or in part, we are looking for something other than God to which we can devote ourselves or through which we can gain acceptance.
> It is one thing to look for meaningful, valuable, satisfying work. It is another to regard work as that which proves to myself, others or God that I

> have worth, that I am acceptable, that my existence is justified. If we depend on our work to give us worth, what happens if we are declared redundant, become invalids or retire? What message do we have for the disadvantaged, the unemployed, the aged?
>
> No, we have to *fully* embrace the gospel which we claim to believe and not just apply it to the need for personal salvation. For it is through Christ's work *alone* that we have worth, find acceptance and know our lives on this earth are well and truly justified. This must be reflected in our attitude to work as well as in our attitude to religious good works.[12]

This quotation is suggestive of a way of translating the doctrine of justification by faith into terms which are powerfully relevant to our daily living. The way in which Romans came alive in the sixteenth century will not necessarily be the way in which it comes alive and seeps into our innermost being today.

Robert Banks, in his book *The Tyranny of Time*, has pointed to one line of application well worth pursuing. There are many more. But first, we must hear Paul in his own terms and to that task we now turn.

Discussion questions

Talking it through

1 What do we expect to gain from studying the book of Romans? Is this the first time you've read it?

2 We should not force our agenda on God — but we often do! How can we properly recognise God's right in setting the entry terms to heaven? What sort of humility does God require? What is the wrong sort of humility?

3 Our minds matter. Besides understanding what Paul actually meant in this letter, how can we use our minds in a constructive way in studying the book of Romans?

4 The most effective way of reading Romans is to see ourselves from God's perspective. How can we do this? Why is it so hard to view life as God does?

5 We often try to 'justify ourselves'. What are we trying to prove? What is the real basis of our worth as individuals?

Widening our horizons

1 Give other examples where hard thinking is required in life. Why do we often short-circuit this process when studying the Bible?

2 Name some books you consider as 'essential reading'. Does it include the book of Romans? Explain why you consider these other books are indispensable.

3 Think of a situation where putting yourself first led you into trouble. What trouble exactly?

4 Self-realisation, self-fulfilment, self-actualisation: these are commonly accepted goals today. Do you have any reservation with these terms?

1
Paul the apostle

Who was Paul and what was his message?

ROMANS CHAPTER 1, VERSES 1 TO 17

PAUL LOSES NO TIME in getting down to business. Right from the start of this letter, he sets out to make the gospel as clear as possible. His opening greeting contains a threefold definition of what he means by 'the gospel'. It is not a vague message of goodwill or a few pious but empty phrases. It is a message whose source is none other than God himself.

Paul: a man with a mission (verses 1 to 7)

Paul didn't invent the gospel. Had it sprung from his own fertile mind, the gospel message would have none of the qualities of permanence and contemporary relevance that men and women have found through the centuries.

❑ *The gospel is the gospel of God — derived from God*

The fact that it had been 'promised beforehand through his prophets in the holy scriptures' (verse 2) is further evidence that it is not the fruit of human musing. Paul, as we shall see in verse after verse of this letter, is an inveterate quoter of scripture. For him, the Old Testament was the word of God and its authority was unquestioned. He looked to it for guidance on many issues and specifically on the way to God.

The good news was no afterthought, but God's eternal plan to bring about human salvation. God had always intended to transform men and women by the way of Jesus' death on the cross. Paul sees this way foretold in the prophets.

❑ *The gospel assures us that God can be trusted*

The fulfilment of Old Testament prophecy is the guarantee not only of the divine origin of the good news, but also of the trustworthiness of God. It is impossible to understand Paul's gospel apart from the Old Testament, but equally it is impossible to understand the Old Testament without relating it to Christ. Taken together, they show that God is true to his word.

This is crucial for the reliability of the message Paul preaches. It is also the reason why in chapters 9, 10 and 11 of this letter he devotes space to a fuller consideration of God's promises to Israel. The veracity of the gospel message was at stake.

❑ *The gospel is centred on Jesus Christ*
He was 'God's Son, who as to his human nature was a descendant of David' (NIV). Paul insists that Jesus shared our nature to the full (see also chapter 8, verse 3). He laid aside his immunity to pain, temptation, suffering and death. He made himself open to all the things that trouble us.

This does not mean, of course, that he experienced everything that actually happens to each one of us. He did not, for instance, experience marriage or old age. But it does mean that his human experience was of such a comprehensive kind as to enable him to understand and feel with us in all situations. As we sing in a well-known Christmas carol:

> And he feeleth in our sadness
> And he shareth in our gladness.

On the other hand, Paul asserts that Jesus was God's Son. What this means is seen in an event that has happened to no-one else in all history — his resurrection from the dead. New Testament scholar C.K. Barrett summarises Paul's thoughts in this way:

> Jesus is all that we are, and all that we are not;

> in him God himself acted in such a way that our world could never be the same again.
> Because Jesus was what he was, we Christians are what we are. Because he is Lord, we are his slaves, owing him total obedience. Because he is holy, we are called to be saints — that is, the holy people of God, marked out for his own possession. Because he is God's Son, there is a gospel and some men (and women) like Paul are set apart for the task of proclaiming it.[1]

Paul: called to work with others in that mission (verses 8 to 16)

In introducing himself, Paul shows what an effect the gospel has had on his own life. Having been brought up as a proud self-righteous Pharisee, he has now become a gentle and tactful Christian.

Paul's call to work with others is shown in two ways:

❑ *Paul's prayer and two-way care*

Paul had never met the Christians at Rome, but they must have warmed to him when they read verses 8 to 15. He prays for them thankfully and consistently. He commends them for their active witness (verse 8), and he longs to strengthen their faith (verse 11).

Another impressive feature of Paul's changed attitude is his willingness not only to give but also to receive from others (verse 12). As Robert Banks has written: '. . .One of the chief dangers inherent in acting as a fulltime helper of other people lies in the development of a helper/helped distinction in one's outlook, one that tends to take hold unconsciously rather than by deliberate choice'.[2]

Paul viewed himself as a helper of others. He also saw himself on the receiving end of their ministry. There was nothing patronising about his attitude.

❑ *Paul's sharing of his zeal*

Along with his prayer and mutual care went all the force of character that, before his encounter with Christ, had made him such a hard man. These verses breathe an air of 'apostolic eagerness' to share the gospel with others. Three successive statements underline this sense of zeal:

* *First,* 'I am bound', 'I am a debtor' or 'I am under obligation' (verse 14). Many, if they engage in evangelism at all, consider that they have conferred a favour upon God and upon his church. But for Paul, sharing the good news was a debt, not a charity. He was bound to it.
* *Second,* 'I am so eager to preach the gospel' (verse 15 — NIV). Paul's eagerness becomes apparent when we see how he longed to get to Rome and had often made plans to do so (verses 11 and 12).

* *Third,* 'I am not ashamed of the gospel' (verse 16). The gospel concerning a little-known, first-century Jewish 'bushie', who lived and worked in cosmopolitan Galilee and died as one among thousands on a cross outside Jerusalem, appears to the world like abject weakness and foolishness. Christians are constantly tempted to be ashamed of it. But not so Paul. In spite of all appearances, this apparently foolish message is supremely powerful.

Key elements of Paul's message (verses 16 and 17)

The apostle continues in the next one-and-a-half verses to give the theme of the whole epistle and the origins of his 'apostolic eagerness'.

Having shown us in the opening greeting how the gospel had changed him, Paul lets us into the secret of its power in verses 16 and 17. Already in verses 2 to 4 we have been given a 'mini-gospel'. Now we are given another which becomes the theme for much of the rest of the letter. The reason for Paul's 'apostolic eagerness' is to be found in three phrases: 'the power of God', 'the righteousness of God' and 'the wrath of God'.

We can summarise the connection between each by saying that 'the power of God' rescues us from 'the wrath of God' by bestowing upon us the 'righteousness of God' when we believe and trust in Jesus. To know that — not simply theologically, but in our own experience — is to be delivered from the temptation to be ashamed of the gospel. It makes us eager to share the good news with others.

❑ *God's power*

Power has become a key topic today among Christians. There is a great deal of enthusiasm about what has been termed 'power evangelism'. In view of this widespread fascination, it is important to be clear on what is meant by power.

Power for Paul is not supernatural brute force. Rather, God's power is directed towards our salvation and, though it includes much more, it has to do with an individual's right standing with God — brought about in such a way as not to compromise God's inner righteousness.

In other words, power for Paul cannot be equated with mere might. These two concepts should never be confused. God's power always has a God-focus, not human-focus, and is consistent with his righteous character and way of working.

❑ *God's righteousness*

This refers *primarily* to a right standing before God and is anchored in the cross. On the cross, the power of God was seen in powerlessness and helplessness. Force was laid aside; sin and evil were borne.

What the cross demonstrates forever is that with God, power is self-giving, and self-giving is power. Theologian Charles Sherlock gives a timely warning when he remarks that 'to focus uncritically on power apart from the cross is to fall into the trap of seeing life — even "spiritual" life — technologically'.[3]

For Paul, 'salvation' includes the important idea of 'being restored to wholeness'. In the higher consciousness or New Age movement, the thought of developing human beings to their full potential has great appeal. The Christian gospel as expounded by Paul has an important contribution to make at precisely this point. Paul goes on to show how the death and resurrection of Jesus opens up the possibility of being restored to the fullness of our relationship with God.

We do not become whole by a process of spiritual osmosis — by surrounding ourselves with intuitive spiritual persons. Until we relate to God, we are not whole and our potential as human beings is not fully realised. The salvation God offers has to do with fullness of life which, we shall see in chapter 8, has implications for both society and the individual.

A right standing before God, offered in the preaching of the gospel, is available to all without *distinction*. Within the framework of basic equality, however, there is a certain *priority* of the Jew — 'to the Jew first and also to the Greek'.

This paradoxical insistence on 'no distinction' and the continuing validity of 'the Jew first' are dealt with at length in Romans chapters 9, 10 and 11 which fall outside the scope of this book. The fact that Paul mentions the Jews in these theme verses shows that the question of God's faithfulness to his ancient people is a significant factor. It has profound implications for the gospel.

If God has not kept his promises to Israel, why should he be expected to keep his promises to Christians today? If Jewish priority was in God's plan and that plan and purpose has been frustrated, then what sort of basis for confidence have we as Christians in God's purpose?

The problem of the Jews is the problem of God. It's as serious as that and cries out for a fuller discussion at some point in this letter. In chapters 9, 10 and 11 Paul will show that God has indeed kept his promises to Israel. It is not Jewish patriotism that constrains him to write these chapters, but the deeper question which undergirds his whole gospel — the question of God's faithfulness.

The priority of the Jews in no way implies that there is one way of salvation for the Jews and another way for the Gentiles. There is one gospel for all, one way of salvation — the way of faith, 'faith from first to last'. Paul supports this statement with a quotation from Habakkuk 2, verse 4: 'The one who is righteous will live by faith.'

Stephen Travis makes the point that Paul's insistence on priority for the Jews does not imply a distinctive way of salvation for them: 'When Jews turn to Jesus in large numbers, they will come to him through faith, during the present course of history. And the return of Jews to Palestine — although it happens under the providence of God and although it could be the prelude to a spiritual turning of Jews to Jesus — is not in itself a specific fulfilment of biblical prophecy.'[4]

The faith of which Paul speaks is not to be regarded as a human work of merit. God is the originator, the creator of faith. Here we have yet another paradox. Theologian James Packer puts it this way:

> Our faith, which from a human point of view is the means of salvation, is from God's point of view part of salvation, and is as directly and completely God's gift to us as is the pardon and peace of which faith lays hold. Psychologically, faith is our own act, but the theological truth about it is that it is God's work in us. . .'[5]

This paradox concerning the relationship between ourselves and God in our justification is difficult to cope with in practice. Paradox seems to many to be nothing more than what E.M. Forster called 'a high-sounding term for a muddle'. Human experience can help us appreciate the place of paradox.

Compare the prayers and the preaching of some evangelists. When they pray, they implore God to convert their hearers (working on the assumption that it is God who does the converting). When they preach, they throw the onus for conversion back on their hearers (working on the assumption that it is a free, human response).

Such practical problems should not lead us to dismiss the paradox as evasive thinking. It is important and acts as a check against two dangerous simplifications of the gospel. First, it excludes the notion that we are mere puppets in the hands of God, that we are coerced into salvation whether we like it or not. Those who adopt a universalist position — the view that everyone will be saved — usually feel that their view implies a kind and generous view of divine action. In fact, the reverse is the case.

What happens, asks Alister McGrath, if someone doesn't want to be saved? 'After all,' he says, 'it is perfectly obvious that at least a substantial part of the human population would regard the idea of being cooped up with God for eternity as something to be avoided at any cost.'[6]

Second, it excludes the notion that we are totally autonomous in accepting or rejecting the offer of salvation. For Paul, a person's salvation is altogether — not *almost* altogether — God's work. Every single factor that gets a person to heaven comes from God.

While there is a human side to every action, there is a divine side as well and the divine side is actually prior to the human side. For the great North African bishop, Augustine (AD 354–430), this was the mystery of prevenient grace — grace that 'goes before' us, preparing the way for us.

It must be admitted that this paradox cannot be explained adequately, but it needs to be recognised if we are to remain faithful to the way in which Paul understands divine and human action in justification. The paradox is a safeguard against distortion of the gospel.

Discussion questions

Talking it through

1 Paul is writing to people he had never met, who are total strangers to him. How does he introduce himself (verse 1)?

2 The Christian gospel is centred on Jesus Christ. Imagine you had only verses 3 and 4 before you to tell you about Jesus. Compose a short creed that summarises the essential facts about him. For example:

We honour Jesus who is. . .

3 Paul knew how to receive as well as how to give. In what practical ways can people mutually encourage one another, building up each other's faith (verse 12)? Give an example of how you have been encouraged by someone else.

4 Paul was keen to see the fruit of the gospel established in Rome (verses 13 and 14). What was this?

5 What is your major task in life? Do you have a single goal that encompasses everything else? If so, what is it? To whose success is this goal directed: your own, other people's, God's — or a combination of all three?

6 Paul in verse 17 quotes Habakkuk chapter 2, verse 4. How is this old truth reminted to make sense of Christ's work on the cross? On what basis does God accept us as holy or righteous? Is this fair?

Widening our horizons

1 How does love for others result in prayer for others and in turn lead to active concern (visiting them, sharing with them, telephoning or writing to them)?

2 What does sharing the gospel represent to you:

a burden?
a duty?
a joy?
a privilege?

Australian author, Dick Innes, says he hates witnessing, but loves communicating. Is there a difference between trying to fabricate circumstances for personal testimony and communicating one's faith naturally? Give an example from your experience.

3 Think of some unlikely candidate to become a Christian — some cynical, prominent or self-centred person. Is God's power great enough to win even them?
Think of some recent public figures who have declared their faith in Christ. What

led to their conversion?
Take some time out now to pray for some public figure you're concerned about and would like to see won into God's kingdom.

4 How is 'the power of God' different from that of:

(a) a politician?
(b) a pop star?
(c) an Eastern mystic?
(d) the cosmos or created order ('May the force be with you')?

Why do you think God has chosen *not* to reveal his power in all circumstances, for example in preventing natural disasters, wars, personal tragedy, terminal illness?

2
The human predicament

Why can't we find God for ourselves?
ROMANS CHAPTER 1, VERSE 18 TO
CHAPTER 3, VERSE 20

ROMANS IS A BOOK which goes against the grain. Whereas the modern trend in theology has tended to be optimistic and self-affirming, convinced that given the proper environment, education and social advantages we will all become better and better, Paul begins his argument by narrating the other side of life — the dark side, the shadow side.

This is the side that most of us do not want to hear about at all, the part that we dare not think about too often or too long. Why not focus upon the *good* news rather than dwell on the bad? Why does Paul, in these opening chapters, enter the cancer ward of the world?

As William Willimon asks in his book, *Sighing for Eden*:

> Why climb Golgotha and look at the world from the Place of the Skull?. . . Why peer into the secret, ugly, 'rag and bone shop' of the heart when there is so much about you and me to be affirmed as good?[1]

The answer, in short, is because that's where the problem lies. Paul begins with the 'gone-wrongness' of human nature because, until we have confronted it, we have not raised the fundamental questions of our existence for which the story of Christ is the only satisfactory answer. Romans details God's answer to our darker side. As much as ever — perhaps even more than ever — it is time to read Romans with new earnestness.

Standing as we do at the end of one century and at the beginning of a new millennia, under the shadow of the mushroom cloud and greenhouse effect, with humanity inching ever closer toward oblivion rather than progress, evil presses itself upon us in new, cosmic proportions.

Paul's cold shower treatment

Here in summary form is Paul's argument as he states it:

1. All men and women, whether Jews or Gentiles, are guilty and inexcusable (chapter 1, verse 18 to chapter 3, verse 20).

2. This universal failure of moral integrity is explained in terms of the solidarity of humankind in Adam. Adam, by rejecting God's specific command, became a sinner. Adam's descendants are born sinners and so sin by nature (chapter 5, verses 12 to 20).

3. Those who are incorporated 'in Christ' do not cease to sin as long as this world lasts. The apostle himself laments the sinful anti-God urges in his heart (chapter 7, verses 7 to 13).

4. Not only human nature, but the whole created universe groans from the effect of sin and its subsequent judgment by God (chapter 8, verses 19 to 23).

Paul will not allow his readers to overlook the seriousness of sin. He realises that what he writes is not flattering to us and that we naturally jib at any view of ourselves which is uncomplimentary. The self-excusing instinct, itself a product of our self-wilfulness (see Genesis chapter 3, verse 12f), is very strong. Three times in the first three chapters, Paul says humanity is culpable. We are guilty!

* Chapter 1, verse 20: 'So they are without excuse'
* Chapter 2, verse 1: 'Therefore you have no excuse. . .'
* Chapter 3, verse 19: 'so that every mouth may

be silenced, and the whole world may be held accountable to God'.

In Jewish law-courts, a person would show that they had no more to say by putting their hand on their mouth. So the holy law of God leaves us with nothing to say in our own defence. We are without excuse.

It needs grace and spiritual enlightenment to believe that our sin is as serious from God's perspective as Paul says it is. We need to ask God to make us humble and teachable when we come to study this theme.

Pleading ignorance is no excuse for disobedience (chapter 1, verses 18 to 32)

After giving a definition of sin (verse 18) and explaining God's revelation of himself to us (verses 19 and 20), Paul provides the following threefold arrangement of his text:

* The failure to make room for God (verses 21-23, 25 and 28a). This leads to. . .
* God's reaction (verses 24a, 26a, and 28a). This in turn leads to. . .
* The downward spiral (verses 24b, 26b and 27, and 28b to 32).

The awesome phrase 'God gave them up' in

verses 24, 26 and 28 is preceded in each sequence by failure to give due recognition to God as the giver of all good gifts. It is followed in each sequence by a progressive moral decline as people become slaves of their own lusts and appetites (verse 24), then are led into greater and greater aberrations (verses 26 and 27) until they become the playground of every heartless and inhuman vice imaginable (verses 28 to 32). This is the way down.

In this passage the nature and seriousness of sin is defined and clarified in three ways:

❑ *Sin exposes us to the wrath of God*

Many of us fail to realise this. It is partly because sin does not incite our own wrath, that we do not believe that sin provokes the wrath of God. The concept seems medieval and barbaric. We cannot, however, dismiss this notion so easily.

In the preaching of the gospel, both the *righteousness* of God (verse 17) and the *wrath* of God (verse 18a) are revealed. It is particularly in the crucifixion of Jesus that we see the full measure of God's holy antagonism towards sin.

God's wrath is not the irrational outburst which so often characterises human anger. With him, wrath does not mean a fit of temper. Our wrath is like that because we are touchy and proud. Anger possesses us and gets out of control so that we regret it later. Even the highest and purest human wrath is a distorted and twisted reflection of the wrath of God.

There are tokens of the active wrath of God to be seen in the disasters befalling humanity in the course of history. The breakdown of communities, split families, rumbling tanks and flashing missiles are not just the automatic effects of our blind wrongdoings. They are, in fact, evidence of God giving us up to our sins — of returning them upon our heads, as the Old Testament puts it.

But the full horror of that anger is seen most clearly before Jesus' crucifixion in the garden of Gethsemane and in the crucifixion itself. God's wrath is his fixed hatred of sin and his determination to act accordingly. It is his righteous attitude to all evil and the mirror-image of his love of all that is good. In his identification with people, Jesus becomes the object of God's holy wrath against sin. As the hour of Jesus' death approaches, the full horror of that wrath is revealed.

As we shall see when we come to the heart of Paul's letter (in chapter 3) and the heart of the gospel, the wrath of God is *averted* by the love of God through the sacrificial offering of the Son of God in our place.

❑ *Sin is an attempt to stifle truth*

In verse 18b, Paul unfolds what we might call a 'psychology of atheism'. There have been many attempts to explain Christian belief in psychological terms.

For instance, the notion of God as Father has been seen as a projection of the human mind. During infancy and childhood we are entirely dependent upon parental care. The adult subconsciously compensates for the loss of this parental care by imagining a heavenly parent who will guard and guide throughout life.

Generally speaking, Christians have seen no good reason to dispute this suggestion. This may well be the psychological mechanism which God uses to bring some people to faith. But in contrast to this widespread awareness of the psychology that lies behind belief in God, there is a woeful ignorance of the psychology of *un*belief. Paul in this passage maintains that unbelief is generated not so much by intellectual causes as by moral and psychological ones.

American author and theologian R.C. Sproul draws attention to the problem in this way:

> It is not that there is insufficient evidence to convince rational beings that there is a God, but that rational beings have a natural hostility to the being of God. In a word, the nature of God (at least the Christian God) is repugnant. . . and is not the focus of desire or wish-projection. Man's desire is not that the omnipotent, personal Judeo-Christian God exist, but that he not exist.[2]

According to Paul in verse 20, God has made a partial knowledge of himself plain in creation. He uses a word play to show that if the pupil doesn't learn, it is not because the teacher didn't teach. The original language makes the word play clear. It can be rendered in English as 'his unseeable things . . . are clearly seen'.

The fault lies not with God, but with humankind. Because of human perversity we try to suppress or stifle that understanding. It is this attempt to suppress the truth which is at the heart of Paul's psychology of atheism.

God's presence is severely threatening to human beings. He threatens our moral standards, our autonomy and our desire for concealment.

He represents the invasion of light into the darkness to which we are accustomed. As a result, we do our best to blot out the truth of God, or at least camouflage it in such a way that its threatening character can be concealed or dulled. Repression, therefore, leads either to atheism or to a kind of religion that makes God less of a threat than he really is. Either way, truth is exchanged for a lie.

We can never ultimately succeed in getting rid of God's truth. It will triumph in the end. The poet, Steve Turner, makes the point in this way:

We say there is no God
(quite easily)
when amongst the curving

steel and glass of our
proud creations.
They will not argue.
Once we were told of a
heaven
but the last time we strained
to look up
we could see only skyscrapers
shaking their heads
and smiling no.
The pavement is reality.
We say there is no God
(quite easily)
when walking back through
man's concerted achievements
but on reaching the park
our attention is distracted
by anthems of birds coming
from the greenery.
We find ourselves shouting
a little louder now because
of the rushing streams.
Our voices are rained upon by
the falling of leaves.
We should not take our arguments
for walks like this.
The park has absolutely no manners.[3]

People are not in the unfortunate position of lacking information. Their claim that God is elusive is an excuse. God is constantly making himself known in creation, but there is a deliberate rejection of the information given. Our thinking has become futile, standing in need of renewal. Later, in Romans 12, verse 2, Paul speaks of 'the renewing of your minds'.

John Wesley used the following prayer in his devotions on Wednesdays. The language is archaic, but the prayer request is always in season:

> O God, whose grace it is that mightily rescues our reason from the desperate rebellion of our passions; grant, we beseech thee, that the experience of the miserable effects of yielding to their allurements may make us warier in observing and severer in repressing their first motions; and let thy grace so strongly mortify us against all their assaults that reason may more and more recover its due force and calmly join with faith to secure and exalt in our hearts the blissful throne of thy love, through our Lord Jesus Christ, thy Son, who liveth and reigneth with thee and the Holy Spirit, one God, blessed for ever. Amen.

❑ *Sin is essentially a form of idolatry*

Paul tells us that the essence of sin consists of a determination to pursue our own independence in defiance of the Creator: 'for though they knew God, they did not honour him as God or give thanks to him' (verse 21). It is a refusal to allow the Creator to be God.

Life is lived by keeping the reins in our own hands and holding God at arms length. We live not for him, but for ourselves — loving, serving and pleasing ourselves without reference to the Creator. Sin is identified in this passage as a revolt against God, a bid for independence.

From this self-deifying attitude spring acts of self-assertion: acts of idolatry against God and inhumanity towards our neighbour.

This section of Romans is usually understood as being addressed to unbelieving Gentiles. They cannot claim to be entirely ignorant of God in view of what can be deduced from the order of creation. We know that Corinth, from where Paul was writing this letter, was rife with idolatry and immorality. The two always go hand in hand. Over a thousand sacred prostitutes were attached to one large temple in Corinth in the first century AD.

But Paul's argument is applicable to Jews as well as Gentiles. His language in verse 23 echoes what is said in Psalm 106, verse 20 with reference to Israel's manufacture and worship of the gold calf (Exodus 32). Neither Jew nor Gentile were entirely free from idolatry and immorality, the twin evils mentioned in this section. The passage lays bare the truth about humankind. Idolatry is to be found in ancient and modern paganism, in Israel, in the church and in the life of each believer. It takes many forms.

One form is that of *religion*. Religion is a great way of keeping God at bay! We politely doff our hats to a distant 'Almighty' and give him what we consider to be 'his due', while firmly barring him from intervention in business, political and personal matters. At other times religion as practised is little more than 'magic', an attempt to tap divine power for our own ends. God is regarded as kind of poker machine, an impersonal power (Lady Luck or Fate) to be played to our advantage.

By honing in on people's love of things, idolatry is as rampant as ever it was in the ancient world. For many, the 'temple' has become the supermarkets and shopping malls of our cities, with their high-priests of advertising and their alluring music to seduce the worshipper. It is no accident that the hit movie *Pretty Woman* was built around the twin pursuits of casual sex and shopping. Materialism is a powerful deity that commands fierce loyalty and ardent devotion.

Sporting centres represent temples for many more adherents of the fitness cult, the body beautiful, who seek to overcome their fear of aging by jogging, dieting and a rigorous program of training. The cult of bodybuilding, with its search for the perfect body, is concerned with much more than looking good. It is about modern society's preoccupation with self-image, with the elevation of the physical over the spiritual, with the glorification of the temporal over the eternal.

Paul's analysis of sin in terms of idolatry is as relevant as ever it was. It is still true today that people give ultimate value to our present human existence, with its totems and status symbols, and 'exchange the truth about God for a lie'. This idolatry brings its own retribution. The English theologian J.A.T. Robinson has rendered the appalling statement 'God gave them up. . .' into popular jargon as 'God lets them stew in their own juice'.

It is not that God reacts to sin by vindictively lashing out against those who refuse to give him his due. It is rather, as Leon Morris has stated, that God pays us the compliment of taking our freedom seriously. He does not constrain us to serve him. But when we choose the wrong, he sees to it that we go along with our choice and that we experience what that choice means.

In failing to make room for God, human nature self-destructs. Irrational thinking, emotional instability, sexual perversion, social chaos and an anaesthetised conscience are the result. The devastating monument to human degradation called 'Auschwitz' did not happen overnight. It was a progressive moral deterioration which led to greater and greater aberrations until any and every deviation became acceptable. Disorientation towards God results in disintegration towards humanity. Evil does not recognise any 'no-go' areas.

For Paul, homosexual intercourse is one manifestation, amongst others, of the disorientation of human life resulting from humanity's rebellion against God. The exchanging of natural relations for unnatural (verses 26 and 27) represents a denial of the Creator's original intentions as set out in Genesis 1, verses 26 and 27:

> 'Let us make humankind in our image, according to our likeness.'
> . . .So God created humankind in his image, in the image of God he created him; male and female he created them.'

God is a relational being ('Let *us* make humankind') and he has created humanity in his own image as relational beings. What this means is spelt out in the Genesis passage in terms of 'maleness' and 'femaleness'. In effect, homosexual acts deny half the image of God. As the apostle sees it, they are 'unnatural', because they do not reflect the fullness of the divine image.

Many today are prepared to concede that homosexual acts fall short of the Genesis ideal, but do not wish to take the further step and claim that such acts call for repentance. The retired Bishop of Birmingham, Dr Montefiore, made the quip: 'My eyesight falls short of an ideal, but it hardly needs repentance!'

Likewise the leaked Osborne Report prepared for

the bishops of the Church of England acknowledges that, while homosexual acts fall short of the biblical ideal, they need not require repentance. The Report alleges that loving committed and trusting relationships between homosexual people, while in some respects sinful and falling short of the pattern of life revealed in the Bible, 'make the best moral sense of a situation which is, of itself, flawed'.[4]

The way in which we determine 'the best moral sense' of this or any other matter is, of course, the key question. Broadly speaking, there are two approaches:

(a) The personalist approach

This approach argues that what is to be done in any situation is that which enhances the quality of personal relationships. So Canon Douglas Rhymes asks: 'If the homosexual is able to find a same-sex partner with whom to share life (and, if the sharing is complete, it will probably include body, mind and spirit), then is that not the most fulfilling and mature way to resolve his or her own needs?'[5]

(b) The prescriptivist approach

This approach agrees that human fulfilment is important, but argues that such fulfilment comes only as God's will is done. This is not to say that God's will is always clear-cut or that individual circumstances are unimportant (that is a third, but unacceptable approach to solving ethical questions — the legalist approach). Individual circumstances are certainly to be considered, but they are to be considered in the light of the Bible. This approach avoids the danger of setting up the individual as an ultimate authority.

Some proponents of the personalist approach are in danger of suggesting that they know better than the Creator what his intentions and purposes were in creation. They are apt to dethrone God and enthrone humanity. Indeed, they can lead us back to the idolatry which was the point of departure for this entire discussion in Paul's letter.

The truth of the matter is that the entire human race stands under the wrath of God. It is not just those engaged in homosexual intercourse. As Lance Pierson has said: 'Romans 2 rounds on the self-righteous homophobe as devastatingly as Romans 1 exposed the militant gay. Romans 3 heaps us all together as sinners under God's judgment.'[6] But the judgment is the instrument of his love. God desires the salvation of humanity enough to get angry about it.

He is angered by any sin that distorts, oppresses or dehumanises humanity. Elizabeth Nance plumbs the pathos of such a caring God in her questioning poem entitled, 'God also died for gays':[7]

Petition going 'round the other day,
  a thousand lines for faithful men to sign.

'Stop the Mardi Gras' — it came my way.
I played the game, I shrugged
  and wrote my name.
But then I wondered. . .
  because I knew God also died for gays.
We're called: Stand up to evil in this world,
  fight injustice, let Christ's voice be heard.
We're called as salt to purify society.
And yet I am still questioning:
Was this an act of faith or plastic piety?
Does the sweeping of my pen condemn
  these people?
Does it bash them, bruise them, bury them,
  pour brimstone from the steeple?
Does this ignore the pleading, dying heart,
  or does the situation really reek?
Is the silence of the church liberal and weak?
Does the scrawling of my name judge and scorn,
  or herald a new purity of dawn?
Does silence help accept the unacceptable,
  or does it condone the morals of this festival?
I'm asking, searching: what would Jesus do?
All I know is God died for gays, too.

Claiming knowledge does not excuse disobedience (chapter 2, verses 1 to 24)

The apostle Paul knew the human mind very well. He understood that it has an infinite ingenuity in making excuses and an almost infinite unwillingness to face the facts and admit guilt.

In Romans 1, verses 18 to 32 he has argued that

no-one can plead ignorance before a holy and just God. There is a universal knowledge of God available to all through creation. It is not a knowledge which is enough to save. It is enough only to condemn and make idolatry inexcusable. Paul now turns in chapter 2 to the second prong of his argument — namely, no-one can plead exemption from obedience on the grounds of knowledge.

Paul appears to have the Jews primarily in mind in verses 1 to 16, though not exclusively so. His concern throughout Romans chapter 1, verse 18 to chapter 3, verse 30 is to show that there is no partiality before God. *All*, whether Jew or Gentile, lack the glory of God. There are self-righteous Gentiles who fail to live up to the knowledge they have, just as there are self-righteous Jews who fail to live up to the knowledge they have.

The key concept in chapter 2 is that of judgment. It is a concept from which the modern world shrinks. Speak today of the love of the Father, the friendship of Jesus, the gifts of the Spirit and you strike a chord immediately. All those ideas are on the same wavelength as contemporary thinkers. But the thought of God as a judge appears repellent and unworthy. But it is necessary for God to judge for a number of reasons:

- *Judgment is an affirmation of the moral character of God*

One of the most oft-heard cries from children at a time of disagreement is 'It's not fair!' Adults make the same complaint in the face of life's inequalities. From childhood we all have a sense that there should be justice in the world and, when it is not experienced, we feel something is seriously out of kilter. If there is a God, we instinctively expect moral perfection of him.

As English theologian James Packer asks:

> Would a God who did not care about the difference between right and wrong be a good and admirable Being? Would a God who put no distinction between the beasts of history, the Hitlers and Stalins (if we dare use names), and his own saints be morally praiseworthy and perfect? Moral indifference would be an imperfection in God, not a perfection. . . The final proof that God is a perfect moral Being, not indifferent to questions of right and wrong, is the fact that he has committed himself to judge the world.[8]

❑ *Judgment is an affirmation of the moral significance of human life*

The idea of judgment brings out human accountability and gives dignity and value to the lowliest action. Our choices have an effect. We may sometimes think that we can believe and do what we like and it will make no difference to ourselves or our relationship with others or God. But that is not, in fact, the way things are.

Responsibility and accountability are part and parcel of what it means to be human. Those who wish to free people from the awesome thought of divine judgment need to remember that they often liberate people into the bonds of meaninglessness and emptiness.

The final two lines of John Braine's novel, *Room at the Top,* make this clear. Joe's folly has ruined his life and the lives of many others, and his friends are trying to comfort him by making light of it all:

> 'Nobody blames you, love. Nobody blames you.'
> 'Oh, my God', I said, 'that's the trouble.'

There is a 'strange comfort' in the thought of God as our judge. It shows God's evaluation of human worth.

- *Judgment assures us that ultimately right will triumph over wrong*

Paul believes it is unthinkable that the present conflict between good and evil should last throughout eternity. Judgment means that evil will be disposed of authoritatively, decisively, finally.

Judgment, then, is a reality to be faced and, Paul argues, there will be no escape from it by those who in their self-righteousness plead their knowledge of God's law — either in the scriptures (Jews) or in their hearts (Gentiles). Like the decadent men and women in Roman society mentioned in Romans 1, the self-righteous — whether Jew or Gentile — are without excuse.

Paul is not limiting his words to Jews. It is not until verse 17 that the word 'Jew' is used. He knows that there is something of the Pharisee in each one of us. His words have application to all who have taken up a position of smug moral superiority. In their self-justifying ways they jack themselves up to their high pedestal. Like the elder brother in the parable of the prodigal son, the self-righteous mind is one that keeps score: 'Father, I have served you these many years. . .'

But as Bishop John Taylor has written:

> The whole doctrine of justification by faith (grace) hinges, for me, upon my painfully reluctant realisation that my Father is not going to be any more pleased with me when I am good than he is now when I am bad. He accepts me and delights in me as I am. It is ridiculous of him, but that is how it is between us.
> In consequence, I want to show my love for him fully and continuously, and I can do that best by insisting on my freedom to push into his presence, grubby and outrageous, without having first to wash my hands and comb my hair.[9]

We are inexcusable: 'all our righteous deeds are

like a filthy cloth' in God's sight (Isaiah 64: 6). Before a righteous and holy judge, we need to admit that and plead for mercy.

Paul applies his message to his readers by changing from the third person plural at the end of chapter 1 to the second person singular in chapter 2. It is a regular way for Paul to say, in effect, 'if the cap fits, wear it'. He applies the message forcefully to the reader. Instead of talking about the whole human race, Paul is talking to us as individuals:

> Therefore you have no excuse, whoever you are, when you judge others; for in passing judgment on another you condemn yourself, because you, the judge, are doing the very same things.

The brand of self-righteousness which Paul is here exposing is based on the faulty logic which goes as follows:

> I don't do what they do (i.e. the decadent Roman pagans in chapter 1), therefore I'm better than them, therefore I'm all right.

But the basic premise is false. Paul insists that those who pass judgment do 'the very same things'. This does not mean that the overt actions are the same, but the covert attitudes are fundamentally similar. It is very difficult to accept sin in ourselves. We either try to cover it over in the hope that others will not see it, or we attempt to shift the blame.

Anyone who has had anything to do with marriage counselling will know that there is virtually no such thing as an 'innocent party'. Marriage counsellor Duncan Buchanan says:

> . . .in twenty-five years, I have only come across one divorce where I believe the one party was genuinely without blame. Yet if one listens to each of the partners talking, one would imagine that, while it is conceded that there might be minor faults here and there, each of the partners sees herself or himself as innocent — and injured. If one unpacks the 'minor faults', one usually discovers a can of worms![10]

In the arena of interpersonal relationships, there is no lack of judgment and criticism, much of which is thoroughly inconsistent. By contrast, the divine judgment is related to truth.

Judgment is actually the moment of truth — a seeing how we really are, measured by that ultimate reality, God himself. It is knowing how I stand before the bar not of economic success, of what neighbours and friends say, or of my own self-image, but before the final truth. Judgment is light showing up the fact of the matter. There will be no misunderstanding, no misrepresentation, no miscarriage of justice and no mistakes — all will be based on truth. As such, it should begin to ring bells for a generation which has set great store by authenticity and personal honesty.

Paul makes it clear that *all* people, Jew and Greek, can anticipate the judgment of God, for no-one will escape. The prevailing philosophy of our society rests on naive assumptions such as 'She'll be right, Jack' or 'I'll take my chances and I think they're as good as the next man's'. People think that somehow they can escape the judgment of God. But there is no escape (verse 3).

Author and journalist Malcolm Muggeridge came to see this:

> However far and fast I've run, still over my shoulder I catch a glimpse of you on the horizon, and then I would run faster and farther than ever, thinking triumphantly: Now I have escaped. But no, there you were, still coming after me. Very well, I'd decide, if I can't get away by running, I'll shut my eyes and ears and not see or hear you. No good! One sees and hears you, not with the eyes and ears, but inwardly with the soul, whose faculties never can be quite put out however gorged, stupefied and ego-inflated they may become. I can flee no further; I fall. Mercy!'[11]

Good works versus 'doing good'

There is one feature about chapter 2 which puzzles many readers in a document whose central message concerns 'God accepting us even though we have done wrong'. It is Paul's claim in verses 6 to 10 that the judgment of God is based on human actions. Unless we are to accuse the apostle of inconsistency, we must think through carefully this apparent contradiction. It is in fact more apparent than real.

'Doing good' (verse 7) and 'doing evil' (verse 9) do not denote good and bad deeds looked at individually and externally. This is brought out by the use of the singular in verse 7. Literally translated the verse reads: 'To those who by steadfast perseverance in the good work seek glory and honour and immortality — eternal life.'

Rather than isolated works, Paul has in mind the entire direction and character of an individual's life. Those who are persistent 'in doing good' are believers; those who are self-seeking and who reject the truth and follow evil are unbelievers. The relevance of our 'doing good' is not that it ever merits a divine reward. It is far too short of perfection to do that. But it does provide an index of what is in the heart — what, in other words, is the real nature of each agent.

The judgment of God is based strictly on the response of the individual to the knowledge of truth that has been made available. There are no favourites or exceptions.

The Jews had many privileges in the divine plan of salvation. But these privileges did not exempt them from the consequences of sin. Their undoubted position of primacy indicated by the repeated expression, 'the Jew first and also the Greek', includes a primacy of judgment. 'The nearer God places anyone to his own light, the more harmful is the choice of darkness.'

If there is no partiality toward the Jews because of their privileged position, it is equally true that there is no partiality to the Gentiles for their lack of privilege. Although the Gentiles do not possess the law as a book in their hands, they do possess it in their hearts in the form of conscience.

The human conscience is not infallible. It may at times be weak, but it is there by nature — not by culture or training. Anthropologists tell us that there are certain tribes who don't think wrong what other tribes do think wrong. And that is no doubt true. Standards vary.

Nevertheless, everybody has a native sense of justice and the judgment of God is based on the light that people have received and their reaction to it. It is never based on the light they have not received. On the last day there will be no appeal against judgment, because everybody will see that God has acted absolutely fairly.

* * *

Paul's purpose in these opening three chapters is to

show that there is simply no way in which we can establish our good standing before God: we depend entirely on his mercy. When every prop is kicked away, we see that we must lean only on God.

In chapter 2, verse 17 Paul turns specifically to the Jewish world. The Jews pride themselves on the knowledge they have and on the moral instruction they give to others. Yet the very law they teach they also disobey. This being so, their privileged status as God's covenant people will not render them immune to his judgment.

We mistakenly assume that knowledge is a substitute for obedience (verses 17 to 24). Parents, for example, sometimes say to their children, 'You must not do that', but they do the very same things themselves. We are apt to think that bringing our children up the right way is a satisfactory alternative to having to practise the right way ourselves. We gain a vicarious satisfaction by approving in other people what we evidently don't approve in ourselves or condemning in other people what we excuse in ourselves.

It is a perverse form of self-deception designed to help us to retain our moral self-respect, while all the time we continue to sin.

The danger that faced the Jews (of failing to live according to their faith) is a danger that confronts all religious people.

Claiming privilege is no substitute for obedience (chapter 2, verses 25 to 29)

Paul then turns his attention to the rite of circumcision (verses 25 to 29). Circumcision was the sign that God himself had given to his people in order to mark them out from others as belonging to him.

First, he had given them the covenant (or agreement) by saying, 'I shall be your God, you shall be my people' and, having given the covenant, he gave them circumcision as a *sign* of the covenant. It was a symbol of their acceptance of God's rule over their lives and their expectation that he would be as good as his word. The mistake that many Jews made was to treat this important sign as a kind of magical charm which would render them immune to the judgment of God.

Again, this is not a mistake which is confined to Jews. There are many people today whose 'folk-religion' borders on superstition. They bring their children for baptism and ask to have them 'done', thinking that they have thereby assured their infants of a first-class ticket to heaven. Folk-religion requires sensitive pastoral procedures but, whenever it affirms the role of merit and salvation-status, it is opposed to the Christian message.

Belonging to God and the people of God is not primarily something outward and physical. It is something inward and spiritual. It is the work of the Holy Spirit in giving us new birth so that, being new people, we live lives of new obedience. Outward signs and sacraments are no insurance against the judgment of God.

Special privilege, special responsibility (chapter 3, verses 1 to 8)

Paul in chapter 3 turns to correct a couple of possible misunderstandings that could be drawn from what he has so far said. In emphasising the inwardness of true religion, the apostle is neither denying the privileges of the Jews (verses 1 and 2) nor accusing God of injustice or unfaithfulness (verses 3 to 8).

From what has been said about circumcision in chapter 2, verses 25 to 29, the answer to the question 'Then what advantage has the Jew?' (3: 1) might be thought to be: 'There are no advantages'. But surprisingly, Paul says exactly the opposite. The Jews have many advantages.

In particular, 'they have been entrusted with the very words of God' (verse 2 — NIV). Whatever their failings, the Jews were God's chosen people. The law he gave was his gracious gift and the rite of circumcision his appointed seal and sacrament. Both had deep significance, despite the fact that the Jews had distorted their true meaning.

Paul touches upon the question of injustice and unfaithfulness only briefly in verses 3 to 8. The question is critical to the whole epistle and is dealt with more fully in chapters 9 to 11. The problem of God's faithfulness to the Jews raises questions about the veracity and reliability of the Old Testament. Has God's whole plan misfired? If God has been unfaithful in keeping the Old Testament promises, why should he be thought to be faithful to his promises to us today in the gospel?

The problem of the Jews, touched upon in this passage, is nothing less than the problem of God. Clearly, Paul's wrestling with this question at length in chapters 9 to 11 is not a digression in the argument of the epistle. It is integral to all that is written.

Nothing can cancel God's faithfulness to us. There is a sense of relief as we read Paul's words in verses 3 and 4, reminding us that our lack of faith in no way alters God's faithfulness towards us! We can always turn to him in prayer and ask him to help our unbelief. Like the man who came to Jesus, we can pray; 'Lord, I believe! Help my unbelief!' (Mark 9, verse 24 — NIV).

Together — before God (chapter 3, verses 9 to 20)

Paul is now ready to bring together the threads of his argument to show the utter inexcusability of the human race. The unrighteous, the self-righteous and the religious are *all alike* guilty before a holy God.

The Jews do have certain advantages as the covenant people of God. But in respect to God's judgment, they have no advantage at all. All are charged with being 'under sin'. As has been well said, 'The awful togetherness of the human race, that takes precedence over every other similarity or dissimilarity, is that before God we are all exposed in our sinfulness.'[12]

In verses 10 to 18, there is a grim list of scriptural quotations from the Psalms and Isaiah to support God's charge. The passages, probably memorised by Paul, remind the reader that this view of humankind is not novel to the author. His position is precisely the position of the Old Testament. This is, and always has been, the way God views sin. The passages make up three strands of evidence which point to the fact that:

* Sin is at the root of the problem of *those who desire to run away from God* (verses 11 and 12). Without exception, the human race has a bent to evil and a bias to disobedience.
* Sin is at the root of the problem of *human speech* (verses 13 and 14). Paul deals with the four organs associated with speech: the throat, tongue, lips and mouth.
* Sin is at the root of the problem of *violence* (verses 15 to 18). The problems of domestic violence and football rampages are modern manifestations of an old problem. Violence lies beneath the surface of our society, because it is beneath the surface of each one of us. Some, by temperament, are

more able to control it. But it's still there.

The string of Old Testament quotations were designed to show that nobody can answer God back. The holy law of God (which in this case includes the Psalms and Isaiah and therefore probably represents the whole Old Testament) leaves us nothing to say in our own defence. If we try to climb to God upon the ladder of our own good works and to make a case before him, all we actually achieve is to discover just how sinful we are!

Paul's thesis is that we have no excuse to offer:

* *We cannot plead ignorance* — the truth has been revealed, but we try to smother it.
* *We cannot plead knowledge* — moral knowledge is not to be studied, but to be obeyed.
* *We cannot plead privilege* — sacramental signs are worthless if the inward reality is missing.

There can be no buckpassing. All that we can do is to join in a prayer which has been made in the church for nearly two thousand years: *Kyrie eleison! Christe eleison!* ('Lord, have mercy! Christ, have mercy!').

It is easy to react to these opening chapters with vehemence, to be incensed by the themes of wrath, sin and judgment and to try to turn down the volume when these truths begin to get through.

This is especially the case among those who are caught up with the human potential movement and 'New Age' groups. While many of these groups employ Eastern ideas, they are also part of a wider and more significant movement within our society, established on the conviction that within each person resides all the potential needed to overcome life's hardships and sorrows.

Although this movement is related to a tradition that was given expression by Mary Baker Eddy, modified by Norman Vincent Peale (author of *The Power of Positive Thinking*) and more recently expounded by Robert Schuller (as possibility thinking), it also has its own gurus. Principal among these are Abraham Maslow, Carl Rogers and Wilheim Reich.

The operating assumption of the movement is the essential innocence of humankind, each member of whom has enormous and untapped capacities for love and constructive behaviour. It is perhaps most transparent in the idea of human OK-ness: 'I'm OK, you're OK'. Rogerian, humanistic psychology said that low self-image rather than sin is our problem. The goal of counselling is to build 'ego strength' in order to enable self-affirmation.

From Paul's perspective, this assumption is naive. Human beings are neither innocent nor a reservoir of untapped spiritual potential. For the New Age people, the divine future is incipiently present in human nature; for Paul it is not.

For the New Age people, what is right and wrong is no longer a moral issue *per se*. Questions of good and evil yield to an analysis of whether an individual's potential will be realised through a given action. For Paul, right and wrong matter. In these opening chapters he makes his point loud and clear. There is a basic 'not OK-ness' in human nature. Our true 'OK-ness', as we shall see in the next chapter, is most deeply experienced through the forgiving and transforming work of Jesus.

The God to be faced is a God of holy love and holy wrath who loves righteousness and hates evil. This is the character of the God from whom we are estranged and with whom we need to be reconciled. Taking seriously God's *God-ness,* his otherness, means seeing ourselves as guilty in the sight of God, whether or not we have guilt feelings; it means being prepared to admit that we cannot spruce up our character so that God will come over to us. We can do nothing even to catch his eye.

Robert Horn illustrates our position by contrasting it with contemporary industrial bargaining processes. He says:

> In industrial relations, both unions and management have some leverage with each other. Unions can call men out; management can fire them. But in our situation before God we have no leverage whatsoever. We cannot do one little thing to put ourselves in the right with him. . .

> by showing us the truth about ourselves, God brings us to despair of all do-it-yourself religion.[13]

Only those prepared to move out of their own fantasy world, admitting how totally applicable Paul's dark picture of sin and guilt is to their own life, can appreciate the sunrise that comes in the next few verses.

Discussion questions

Talking it through

1 We need to learn about sin (pages 43 and 44). Do you think we need to practise sin actively to understand it?

2 Do all people know God enough to honour him as Creator (chapter 2, verses 19 and 20)? Can people be ignorant enough to be excused from honouring him at all? Are there degrees of ignorance and responsibility?

3 How is God's anger different from:
(a) My anger at an injustice done to *me*?
(b) My anger at an injustice done to *someone else*?
(c) My anger at an injustice done to *God*?

4 'God pays us the compliment of taking our freedom seriously' (page 55). What is encouraging about this?
What is frightening about it? How do you see personal freedom: as an inalienable right, as a gift or as a responsibility?

5 Read Romans chapter 1, verses 26 to 28. How is obedience to God linked to sexual relationships? *Why* does one affect the other?

6 What bearing do Paul's comments on first century Jewish and Gentile Christians have on each of the following today:
(a) Western and Third World Christians?
(b) Christians who are baptised and those who are not?
(c) Those who are Christian by name and those who are Christian by conviction?

Widening our horizons

1 What is the thinking that lies behind each of these expressions?

(a) The liberation of the children of God
(b) Liberation theology
(c) Free love
(d) Black liberation
(e) Women's liberation
(f) Liberty, equality, fraternity

What elements of these ideas are authentically Christian and what are not?

2 How can the following legitimate interests or activities become an idol?:

(a) Television
(b) Sport
(c) Physical fitness
(d) Leisure
(e) Children
(f) Car

3 What particular forms of idolatry are most likely to affect:

(a) A politician?

(b) A self-employed businessman?
(c) A chronically-ill person?
(d) A person involved with home duties?
(e) A teenager?

4 How can the following be the beginning of a 'downward spiral' (page 46)?
(a) The exercise of power as the chief motivation for work
(b) Failure to honour a debt
(c) A tendency to agree with everyone rather than stand by a strongly-held conviction

5 How do you think God might view:
(a) Anti-corruption inquiries?
(b) Protests at the degradation of the environment?
(c) Attempts to address international, national and personal debt?

6 Many people believe what matters most is 'what is important to me' (the personalist approach to ethics). How can this apparently universal truth conflict with the Christian idea of:
(a) Right and wrong?
(b) Absolute truth and human rebelliousness?

3
God's solution

What does God offer needy humanity?
ROMANS CHAPTER 3, VERSES 21 TO 31

'PEOPLE HAVE AN INTENSE LONGING to be made right,' writes LeRoy Aden. 'They may want to get right with themselves, others, and/or with God, but in any case they feel, however vaguely, that there is something wrong with them and they desire, however fervently, to become acceptable.' [1]

How has God reached out to us?

When there is no belief that God initiates atonement for humankind, then one has to develop one's own survival strategies. Such self-atoning strategies may go in two opposite directions.

Some people, as we saw in the last chapter, try to be made right through their own efforts at good, noble, even religious works, so that their praiseworthy performance will bring them the validation they seek. Others turn against themselves in negative and self-destructive ways as though self-negation and the crucifixion of their own personalities will provide an acceptable atonement to get them into the relationships that they desperately seek.

At such times, it is critical to recall that, underneath all the good works we are proud of and the egoistic attempts to be superhumanly good, there is a fundamental longing to be made right with the ultimate source of life.

This longing, Paul tells us in this passage, can become a reality when it is grounded, not upon our hidden potential, but upon Christ and what he has achieved on the cross. On the cross, God became involved to ensure our acceptance. He is not afraid of getting dirty hands because he genuinely cares for us. 'God wades knee-deep in the rushing water of human adversity and hatred and is rejected and abused by humanity because God cares.'[2]

Commentators on Romans agree that this passage is one of the most important ever written. It is the very heart of the letter, for it sets out God's answer to the problem of human sin. The 'but' here is a major turning point: through the black storm-clouds of God's wrath, the bright light of his fervent love, compassion and passion shine.

God is a God of love and all that he has done,

is doing and will do is done out of love. There is no way we can put ourselves in a position in which God no longer loves us. Nothing that we have done or will do can lose his love.

What is God's righteousness? (verses 21 to 23)

The phrase 'righteousness of God' refers to God's way of putting unrighteous people right with himself. According to Martin Luther, it refers 'not so much to goodness as God-acceptedness'.

We are just not able to achieve this right relationship; we are unable to keep the requirements of God's law. The law, as we shall see more fully in chapter 7, only serves to expose our sin. It cannot rescue us from sin. On the other hand, the fact that the law and the prophets bear witness to faith as the way to get right with God indicates that it is not a new-fangled idea invented by Paul. In essence, it is very old.

Verses 21 to 23 make clear three points about the phrase 'the righteousness of God':

❑ *God's righteousness refers to a right standing before God, which is a present possibility*

This fact is brought out by the 'now' in verse 21. The Jews thought there could be no assurance of a right standing before God until the day of judgment. Paul makes a radical modification to such contemporary Jewish thought by asserting that, for the believer, there is a sense in which the judgment has already taken place: 'Therefore, since we are justified through faith, we have peace with God' (chapter 5, verse 1). The judgment is no longer simply in the future: it has become a verdict *within* history.

Through Christ, God has acquitted those who have faith and there is 'therefore now no condemnation' (chapter 8, verse 1). The age to come has reached back into the present age and opened up the possibility of a qualitively different mode of existence. The future is already penetrating the present. Such is the heart of Paul's gospel. The 'power of God for salvation to everyone who has faith' (chapter 1, verse 16) is now operative and resident in history.

❑ *God's righteousness refers to a right standing before God — wholly undeserved and embarrassingly free*

All of us are guilty, inexcusable sinners — a point made earlier. Paul further underlines his conviction with the words 'since all have sinned and fall short of the glory of God' (verse 23). If we are to be put right with God, it can only be by the free gift of his sheer mercy and grace — the point made in verse 24, where he says that we are 'justified [declared to be in a right standing with God] *freely* by his grace' (NIV) or 'as a gift' (NRSV). It is *gratia* — all for nothing.

This can be offensive to our pride: to live on charity is humiliating. Paul Tournier goes to the nub of the problem with the notion of grace:

> In the last resort this wounds our self-love, this receiving of what we do not deserve. And this is why we have difficulty accepting it. We would prefer to have merited it; we contend with God for the merit.[3]

We have no hold on God whatsoever. He has acted freely — out of sheer grace.

❑ *God's righteousness is only free for us because it was obtained at infinite cost — by God, through Jesus Christ, on the cross*

It is free, but it is not cheap. The way in which Jesus' death on a cruel cross two thousand years ago affects us today has never been made the subject of dogmatic definition. The church has maintained a certain agnosticism about what might be called the 'mechanics' of atonement, while speaking consistently of the *fact* of what was achieved by God in Christ.

We must abandon any pretence to finality in our understanding of the significance of the cross. Paul would concede that we could never plumb the full depth of its meaning. God's actions on our behalf stagger our imagination. Nevertheless, Paul ransacked his vocabulary in order to try to bring out a tiny fraction of what he saw to be that meaning.

Why did Jesus die on the cross (verses 24 to 26)?

There are three powerful symbols which are packed into verses 24, 25 and 26. Paul saw Jesus' death as a *redemption*, a *propitiation* and a *demonstration* of the justice of God.

The power of these metaphors derives from their relationship to everyday life, but tragically over time they have become 'doctrine' and died as images. To communicate this good news today, we need to bring doctrine back to life as image, finding contemporary expressions of release, acceptance and justification which can put people in touch with God.

❑ *The cross is a redemption from slavery (verse 24)*

We are familiar today with hijackings, kidnappings and hostage-takings in which innocent people are required to pay exorbitant ransoms to release innocent captives. In Paul's day, the word 'redemption' was regularly used in the marketplace for the liberation of slaves.

A slave would save his meagre earnings until he had amassed a certain amount — a *lutron* or ransom price. When he had the required amount, he would take it along to the Temple and deposit it there. If he were lucky, he could then go free.

There were a variety of ways in which this process operated in antiquity but, however it was used, the word 'redemption' always denoted two things:

* It meant *deliverance from some serious plight* — whether slavery, condemnation or captivity.
* It meant *payment of a ransom price.* Redemption signified deliverance at a cost.

Paul saw this commercial metaphor as a useful way of bringing out one fact about the cross: there is a more serious form of slavery than physical slavery. As St Augustine wrote in his famous confessions:

> . . .at times a man's slave, worn out by the commands of an unfeeling master, finds rest in flight — whither can the servant of sin flee? Himself he carries with him wherever he flees. An evil conscience flees not from itself; it has no place to go to: it follows itself. Yea, he cannot withdraw from himself, for the sin he commits is within. He has committed sin to obtain some bodily pleasure. The pleasure passes away: the sin remains. What delighted him is gone: the sting has remained behind — evil bondage.[4]

We are prisoners of our self-centredness and from this evil bondage no-one can ever hope to buy his or her own release. Jesus Christ has paid the price that needed to be paid — so that we might be liberated. Our redemption was not won with effortless ease. It was won at a great price. We have no way of measuring the cost involved:

> We do not know, we cannot tell
> what pains he had to bear. . .

❑ *The cross is a propitiation, averting the wrath of God (verse 25)*

Both the NRSV and NIV translations of this verse use the expression 'a sacrifice of atonement' and make no reference to propitiation. But the Greek word involves the idea of dealing with wrath. If we choose to translate the word in another way, we nevertheless need to safeguard the truth that the wrath of God has been turned away from those who have faith in Jesus.

It is easy to object to this image without taking the trouble to understand the *way* in which it is used in the New Testament. Kenneth Stevenson, in his book on the eucharist, is a typical example of this common failure. He writes:

> If propitiation has any right to a place in the Christian vocabulary, it belongs exclusively as a view of the atonement only insofar as it helps to express passion, feeling, power, rather than that Christ actually makes the Father forget his anger at us.[5]

But who said that propitiation is about 'Christ making the Father forget his anger at us'? Certainly not Paul. The crude notion that a kind, second person of the Trinity steps in between sinful humanity and an angry God, rescuing the former from the latter, is a scholarly caricature of Paul's teaching. Paul was never in any doubt that the whole process of propitiation sprang from the heart of a loving God.

Paul saw in this notion, taken over from the pagan temples, yet another piece of the complex jigsaw of what God did in Christ on Calvary. In taking this notion over, however, Paul is careful to disinfect it of its pagan associations. He cleans up the concept so that at three important points it stands in marked contrast to the heathen notion:

* *The wrath of God is his holy displeasure at evil.* It is different from the wrath of the bad-tempered, capricious heathen deities. For them, wrath means 'seeing red'. It is to be out of control.
* *The initiative is with God himself.* Verse 25 states, 'God put forward [Jesus] as a sacrifice of atonement' — more accurately, 'a propitiatory sacrifice'. On the cross, the destructive power of sin is cauterised by the consuming fire of God's love. In the pagan religions, the worshippers took the initiative in bringing their offering to placate their bad-tempered deities.

* *God gave himself in the person of his only Son,* whereas heathen offerings consisted of sweets, birds, beasts, spices and such like. It's not that God 'made' propitiation. He *is* the propitiation. The mention of 'faith in his blood' in verse 25 makes many modern readers uncomfortable. Certain theologians have been quick to dismiss what they have called 'the gospel of gore.' But the mention of blood serves to underline the atrocious physical suffering involved in the crucifixion of Jesus.

The physical pain involved has been described in this way:

> Nothing could be more horrible than the sight of this living body breathing, seeing, hearing, still able to feel, and yet reduced to the state of a corpse by forced immobility and absolute helplessness. . . stripped of his clothing, unable even to brush away the flies which fell upon his wounded flesh, already lacerated by the preliminary scourging, exposed to the insults and curses of people who can always find some sickening pleasure in the sight of the tortures of others. . . torture, degradation, certain death, distilled slowly drop by drop. It was an ideal form of torture.[6]

Paul and the other New Testament writers make no attempt to play on the heartstrings of their readers. They pass over the whole shocking affair with the utmost reserve. It was the meaning of the death, rather than the death itself, which was so important to them. Among other things, it was a way of averting the wrath of God.

With these three important qualifications, the notion of propitiation in the Bible can be seen to be very different from the pagan idea of getting back into the 'good books' of the gods by what really amounted to a process of bribing them. Christian propitiation (as distinct from pagan propitiation) declares that it is God's love that averts God's wrath from us and that it is precisely in the averting of this wrath that we see what real love is.

The early Christians gathered to worship and adore their risen Master with an astonished gratitude. They were vividly aware of an abysmal need which had been met by him on the cross. The recognition that God in Christ bore the brunt of his own wrath against sin put a new depth, realism and vigour into their praise and worship. Their pulse-rate quickened as they recalled the marvellous love of God, demonstrated in the sacrificial death of Jesus.

It is easy to think of the love of God as being as natural and self-evident as gravity. 'Of course God is love,' we say and we are only inclined to question this axiom when we are faced with suffering. *Then* we ask: 'Why does a God of love permit such suffering?'

Our assumption appears at certain perplexing points to be open to question. But it's important to notice that we start with this assumption.

The Bible never claims that God's love is self-evident. It is not a 'truth of natural theology', an insight which we may gain by looking at the night sky, a glorious sunset or the crashing ocean waves. We learn God's love through the cross, not by any other means. It is a truth which causes the New Testament authors to catch their breath in amazement and in an ecstasy of total wonder.

The famous words of Charles Wesley express this recognition:

> Amazing love! how can it be
> that thou, my God, shouldst die for me?

❑ *The cross is a demonstration of justice (verses 25 and 26)*

We have a fierce and primeval inclination towards fairness. It manifests itself early enough in our shrieking protests in the sandbox when our playmate has the shovel for longer than we do, or at the party when his piece of cake is bigger than ours. There is an energy at work in human imagination which suggests that you shall not have more than I.

The cross demonstrates that our childhood cry for fairness corresponds with what we find in the inner being of God. There *is* justice at the heart of the universe.

Paul, seizing upon any word which would help him bring out something of the vast meaning he saw in the cross, turns to legal terms. His concern is to safeguard the inner righteousness of God. Nothing less than the veracity of God is at stake. The fact that he had forgiven sins under the old covenant, although no adequate reparation had been made, had looked like unrighteousness on the part of the divine Judge.

But Paul insists that God's integrity is unimpaired because the sins committed by God's people before the incarnation were not disregarded. Rather they were put on Jesus' account (so to speak), to be atoned for in due course by his death. This was, presumab-ly, how Abraham experienced the joy of justification before Christ came (see Romans 4, verse 3). The punishment of sin committed in the past had been passed over in the divine forebearance.

But, although God could postpone punishment temporarily, he could not postpone indefinitely this backlog of judgment. It could not be brushed aside as though it didn't matter. God cannot simply say, 'let bygones be bygones'. That would amount to God saying that sin does not matter. He would destroy himself because he would undermine his divine character as one who is intrinsically righteous.

It is easy to get the important questions around the wrong way. We are perplexed by the thought of God punishing sin and so we ask, 'How can God be righteous if he does *not* forgive?' But Paul is troubled as to *how* can God forgive? The question for him is: 'How could a righteous God forgive unrighteous people without involving himself in their unrighteousness?'

These two different approaches can be summed up as follows: 'Forgiveness, which to us is the plainest of duties, is to God the profoundest of problems.'

Paul sees the cross as the solution to this divine dilemma. Although in forebearance God temporarily left sin unpunished, now in justice he has punished it. Sin has been condemned in Jesus Christ.

In the light of the cross, nobody can accuse God of injustice or of condoning evil. The cross demonstrates with equal vividness God's holy antagonism towards sin and his infinite love towards sinners. He is able to accept us as righteous in his sight without compromising his own righteousness — because the penalty of sin has been borne by himself in the person of his Son.

The cross shows that God is righteous in his innermost being. In effect, it is his righteous way of 'righteoussing the unrighteous'. No longer can anyone say that God bends his rules or lowers his standards.

Paul brings together in a single sentence these

difficult concepts of redemption, propitiation and justification. We should not be surprised that human language is incapable of conveying the significance of this event in its totality. Leon Morris is right to remind us that 'the human predicament is complex, and God's saving act that deals with that predicament is correspondingly complex.'[7]

One thing is crystal-clear. The good news of what Jesus achieved at Calvary means that the notion of self-salvation is abolished. The struggle to achieve God's favour by our own efforts is at an end.

What does God's solution mean? (verses 27 to 31)

Paul concludes this central core of his letter by drawing out three implications:

* *Boasting is excluded* (verses 27 and 28). It is a curious thing that a person who says, 'I know I am forgiven by God', is sometimes thought arrogant. For Paul, the real arrogance lies in supposing that we can make ourselves good enough to stand before God. God has accepted us on the basis of the cross as a free gift. We have done nothing to deserve it. We deserve only judgment. All boasting is excluded.
* *Discrimination is excluded* (verses 29 and 39). The cross fosters unity. In the gospel, God has given to all the same chance of salvation.

* *Licence to sin is excluded* (verse 31). In Romans chapter 6, Paul will consider more fully the case of those who think that, because God's grace is displayed in forgiving sins, they can go on sinning — on the principle that the more they indulge themselves, the more grace will be poured out.

  For the moment Paul simply asserts that justification is not license to sin. On the contrary, if God has declared us to be in a right relationship with himself, he is committed to taking us forward in grace and we are committed to going on with him in obedience. The cross is an *incentive* to holy living.

It should be noted that by the word 'law' Paul usually means the specific divine requirements given to Israel through Moses. Here we have one of the few instances where Paul may be using 'law' in the broader sense of 'the Old Testament scriptures as a whole'. Such ambiguity is not surprising, since divine legislation ('law' in the narrower and more common sense) is contained within the scriptures ('law' in the broader sense).

Discussion questions

Talking it through

1 Justifying ourselves. How do we seek to do this:

(a) in everyday conversation?
(b) to ourselves?
(c) before God?

2 God's righteousness is sometimes likened to that of a judge who steps down to take the punishment of a convicted criminal. In what way does this example powerfully demonstrate the radical difference between Christianity and other religions? How did God do this?

3 Why don't we need to placate God as if he were an angry, offended deity? In what way is God's wrath different from human anger? How does God's love avert God's wrath? (See pages 89 to 91.)

4 How does the cross of Christ answer the universal cry, 'It's not fair'? What does the cross say about God's love?

5 Does forgiveness mean condoning evil or wrongdoing?

(a) In what way can we presume on God's forgiveness?

(b) Is God under any obligation to forgive us?

(c) What is the clearest sign of forgiveness?

6 Look at the three 'implications' (pages 96 and 97) of being forgiven. What is the most common trap to fall into, do you think? Why?

Widening our horizons

1 Fairness is a slippery concept. Is it really fair that an innocent man (Jesus) was punished for the guilty (us)?

2 'I don't owe anyone anything. I'm free to make my own decisions.' True? If not, why not?

3 Both C.S. Lewis (in *The Great Divorce*) and M. Scott Peck (in *People of the Lie*) suggest that God doesn't punish us, but we punish ourselves. Consider:

> There are only two kinds of people in the end: those who say to God, 'Thy will be done,' and those to whom God says, in the end, '*Thy* will be done.' All that are in hell, choose it (C.S.Lewis, *The Great Divorce,* Collins, 1979, p.66).

> The point is that God does not punish. To create us in his image, God gave us free will. To have done otherwise would have been to make us puppets or hollow mannequins. Yet to give us free will, God had to forswear the use of force against us. We do not have free will when there

is a gun pointed at our back. It is not necess arily that God lacks the power to destroy us, to punish us, but that in his love for us he has painfully and terribly chosen never to use it. In agony, he must stand by and let us be. He intervenes only to help, never to hurt.
The Christian God is a God of restraint. Having forsworn the use of power *against* us, if we refuse his help, he has no recourse but — weeping — to watch us punish ourselves (M. Scott Peck, *People of the Lie*, Century Hutchinson, 1988, p.204).

4 Large-scale criminals are often desperate for social acceptance. How is social acceptance different from peace of mind?

5 Forgiveness is a grace to be given as well as a gift to be received. How can we apply it to the following situations?
(a) Not overcharging a customer or client
(b) Not lying to our wife/husband about an extra-marital affair
(c) Being generous to the needy.

6 What about situations where we have a social obligation to others. Does our forgiveness mean that a person necessarily avoids the civil consequences of his/her crime, e.g. in the case of child abuse, embezzlement or fraud? Why not?

7 How do the following affect your view of the love of God?

(a) The Jewish holocaust

(b) The grinding poverty of Somalia and Ethiopia, both torn by civil war

(c) A train accident/ferry disaster/cyclone/ other 'acts of God'.

4
Genuine faith

What is true faith like?
ROMANS CHAPTER 4, VERSES 1 TO 25

❦

SO FAR, WE HAVE LOOKED at three questions: Who was Paul and what was his message? Why can't we find God for ourselves? What does God offer needy humanity? In chapter 3, verses 21 to 26, Jesus' death was shown to be the *grounds* upon which our relationship with God is founded. In chapter 4, faith is highlighted as the *means* by which that new relationship is served. Paul now uses the life of Abraham to illustrate what true faith is like.

Because of his tenacious, God-honouring adherence to God's promise, Abraham is put forward as the example and pattern for the kind of faith God expects of us. Paul develops this argument by looking at various facets of true faith.

True faith excludes false pride (verses 1 to 8)

Paul has stated in chapter 3, verse 27 that boasting is excluded because of the cross. Now he turns to consider one person who in traditional Jewish thinking may have had some grounds to indulge in a little boasting. If bragging was right for anyone, it was surely right for the revered ancestor of the Jews, Abraham!

In Genesis 26, verse 5 God had said of him: 'Abraham obeyed me and kept my requirements, my commands, my decrees and my laws' (NIV). Even so, Paul states, Abraham has no grounds for boasting before God.

The logic of this chapter is hard, even tedious for Western minds to follow. Paul is arguing in Jewish terms with readers who would find fault with his argument. He is trying to show from the Old Testament that Abraham's acceptance with God came through his faith, not his 'works'. In verse 3, Paul quotes Genesis 15, verse 6 to show that faith itself is not a meritorious work: 'Abraham believed God, and it was credited to him as righteousness' (NIV).

The Jews, however, interpreted this passage quite differently. For example, one rabbi linked faith with merit in this way: 'Our father Abraham became the heir of this and of the coming world simply by the merit of the faith with which he believed in the Lord.' Faith is explicitly understood as a merit or good work deserving of God's favour.

But for Paul, faith is not something *we* produce to earn merit for ourselves. Rather faith is our *response* to God's act of grace. It is God's grace that saves us. Our faith is simply the key that opens the door to that grace, God's undeserved favour.

This point is not always appreciated even by Christians. Many personal testimonies seem to think of faith as, quite wrongly, a 'work'. Christians claim that they have been accepted by God because of what *they* have done: 'Because *I* surrendered. . . Because *I* have decided to follow Jesus. . . Because *I* went to the front at the close of the meeting. . . Because *I* gave my life to Christ'. Yet true faith is an exclusive, wholehearted trust in another, a placing of our entire confidence in God's mercy. Our confidence is *never* in ourselves!

The use of the verb 'credited' in verses 3 to 5 is a technical way of saying that God *gives* us this standing. It is not something we can reach on our own. It is given and it is *free*. Paul pictures a person who has performed an agreed task according to a contract. Such a worker can expect compensation — in the form of a wage credited as 'something owed' (verse 4).

But the person who has not worked has no just claim for compensation. If anything is to be 'credited', it can only be on the basis of pure favour — of grace. Abraham was such a person. All he could do was to humbly place his trust in a God of grace. We have no automatic right of entry.

Paul turns to another Old Testament heavyweight, King David, to further substantiate this principle. He quotes Psalm 32, verses 1 and 2 which contains a key concept. The blessing of acceptance and forgiveness which David experienced came about because his sin was *not* 'counted against' him.

We can see from these two Old Testament illustrations that God's ministry of 'crediting' or 'reckoning' has both a positive and negative aspect. On the positive side, he credits us with righteousness, a right relationship with himself, even though we don't deserve it. On the negative side, he declines to credit sin to those who have broken his law — when they come to him in faith.

American preacher Stuart Briscoe has a pertinent comment on this ministry of 'not crediting':

> Those who find sin relatively unimportant find little difficulty in expecting that human effort, however half-hearted, may well merit forgiveness, but those who know what sin is also know that only divine action can deal with it.[1]

The forgiveness of God is a gift to be received, not a reward to be merited. Righteousness, acceptance, forgiveness — none are earned. They do not become ours by 'doing' or 'labouring', but by 'receiving' or 'believing'.

As far as Paul is concerned, the Old Testament scriptures make it quite clear that neither Abraham nor David had anything to boast of before God. Neither could take credit for having gained acceptance with God by their own efforts. There was no place for boasting before God.

Nothing is more unbecoming in the Christian life than pride. Nothing is more attractive than humility.

True faith is sealed by sacraments (verses 9 to 12)

The Jews had failed to learn an obvious lesson from the history of Abraham. According to the Old Testament, the chronological sequence of Genesis chapters 15 to 17 was as follows:

Abraham justified by faith (Genesis 15, verse 6)

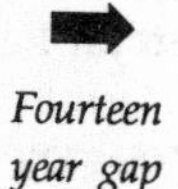

The institution of circumcision (Genesis 17, verses 10 to 30)

Abraham's experience of justification happened fourteen years before his experience of circumcision. Obviously, then, he was not justified *because* he was circumcised. Justification is not even conditional upon circumcision. Therefore, Paul concludes, when it comes to justification, God is not interested in whether or not a person is circumcised, but whether or not a person has *faith*.

This does not mean that circumcision has no value. It was a seal or a symbol, assuring Abraham that the faith he had in God's promise was accepted by God. But it was neither an excluding, nor a contributing factor to his actual acceptance by God.

It is a wonderful thing to be a member of a family that goes back to Abraham and that extends across the world. Abraham's circumcision was a 'badge' of faith that linked him to the circumcised. But being a Jew is neither necessary nor sufficient for justification. The sole condition, open to all, is faith.

The sealing of that faith in outward visible signs is something that applies in both the Old and New Testaments. Just as a wedding ring symbolises the commitment of one person to the other, so it is with other signs. They indicate that whoever has faith has received what God has promised.

As English theologian J.I. Packer says, 'presenting the hood at graduation assures the student that he really has secured his degree'. In chapter 6, Paul will speak of baptism as a 'life-shaper' which can be used as fuel for obedience. As far as he is concerned, it is the *meaning* rather than the *event* which is of ongoing importance. The event belongs to the past and memory of it soon fades.

What is important for the apostle is the ongoing meaning of baptism. It is a graphic symbol of a living faith in Christ that continues beyond the actual experience of baptism.

True faith spells the end of legalism (verses 13 to 17a)

If Abraham did not earn salvation by being circumcised, neither did he earn it by keeping the law! In fact, as Paul points out, if law-keeping was the way to the promised 'inheritance' (no longer representing merely the land of Palestine, but the blessings of salvation), then there could be no guarantee that anyone would be heirs of the promise.

No-one ever satisfactorily keeps the law. Only Jesus Christ has a claim on God on the basis of obedience. For everyone else, there would be only the prospect of total failure.

This is no theoretical matter. It is a line of thought that gets many Christians into difficulty. It affects the person who fears that their Christian commitment is in doubt because their faith is shaky: 'If only my faith were stronger, then I'd be sure. If I try harder, I'll make it.'

Attention is all on the state of faith, the extent of self-effort. Such a person is falling for the fallacy of thinking that it all depends on *them* — the very opposite of saving faith. Such self-absorption ultimately leads to a lack of assurance. We can set out Paul's rather compressed argument as follows:

On our side:
God's plan depends solely on faith,
not the fulfilment of the law, so that. . .

On God's side:
God's gift of salvation may be
a matter of grace, so that. . .

On God's side:
God's promise may not be an empty promise,
but be sure of fulfilment.

If law-keeping had played a part in the claim to the promised inheritance, it would have had two disastrous effects:

First, it would have altered the structure of the divine-human relationship from a 'promise-trust' model to an 'employment-reward' model. Verses 4 and 5 make the difference clear. Verse 15 shows that, because of sin, the keeping of the law would have been perverted into legalism, provoking God's wrath.

Second, a law-keeping basis for the promise would restrict the promised inheritance to the Jews, whereas God's plan included all nations. Paul in verse 17 claims Abraham for the whole human race: 'I have made you a father of many nations.'

True faith goes beyond reason (verses 17b to 22)

Paul has been insisting that Abraham's acceptance by God was not due to religious rites such as circumcision or adherence to the law, but due to his faith alone. But what was his faith like?

There are many ideas abroad today about faith. Often they bear no resemblance to what the Bible teaches about the essential nature of faith. In this passage Paul sets out the characteristics of Abraham's faith — both in *form* and *content*.

❑ *The form of Abraham's faith*

Abraham acknowledged the existence of God but, more than that, he believed God. He trusted him and cast himself totally on God's wisdom, promise, grace and power. Faith is essentially trust in a person — *the* Person, God himself. It begins only when we come to an end of ourselves.

Abraham came to an end of himself, for he could not conjure up the son God had promised him when Sarah was too old. It was when he recognised his hopeless need that Abraham began to trust and have confidence in the living God. And that is always the *form* true faith takes.

The fact that Paul tells us that Abraham 'did not waver through unbelief. . . being fully persuaded that God had power to do what he had promised' (verses 20 and 21 — NIV) needs careful interpretation. We must keep in mind the huge time span that separated the promise in Genesis 15, verse 5 and its fulfilment in Genesis 21, verse 2.

We know from the Genesis account that Abraham was tempted to say, as we might in similar circumstances, 'Well, forget it.' Abraham's faith could at times be described more in terms of struggle, like this prayer of a broken pastor:

> I am hurt, Lord
> I don't want courage or a blithe spirit,
> or faith or hope or charity.
> I don't want to fight or even stand and turn
> the other cheek to fate.
> I want to run;
> to cringe first and then run and hide myself at
> the back gate of hell, despairing, flatly wrinkled
> like a pricked balloon.
> I'm hurt, Lord.
> Don't quote Holy Writ to me.
> Don't even say: 'Lo I am with you.'
> I know all that and it doesn't matter
> for the moment.
> Just hold me, Lord tight-fisted, with a grip like
> all eternity.
> You do it — I can't hang on, not even with one
> finger.
> I, to whom some others run for counsel and the
> handclasp of faith and hope and charity.
> Hold on, Lord. It will pass, but for the moment
> hold.

Faith for Abraham was not automatic or easy. He had struggles just as the rest of us. Paul knew his Old Testament well enough to be sure of this.

Leon Morris cuts through the difficulties we have in identifying with Abraham's apparently serene and undoubting faith when he writes: 'Paul is referring to the settled attitude that endured all this, not to Abraham's initial reaction. The unbelief was momentary, the faith constant.'[2]

❑ *The content of Abraham's faith*

But it is possible to have the form of faith, but lack the *content* of it. This is the case, for example, when we encourage a friend facing problems by saying, 'Don't let go your faith.' We mean: 'Don't give up. Don't lose heart.' We look for an attitude of trust divorced from any corresponding *object* of trust.

Abraham's faith was exemplary because it was clearly related to his knowledge of its object. He knew two things about his God whom he trusted.

God is a God who makes the creation and re-creation of life happen! The God Abraham worshipped was the one Paul said gives life to the dead (verse 17b). Paul probably has two facts in mind when he speaks of Abraham believing in such a God:

(a) Abraham's personal circumstances

Advanced in years, his generative powers were 'dead' and Sarah his wife was experiencing similar 'deadness' in her womb. Frankly, it was a hopeless situation. Nevertheless, Abraham believed 'against all hope' (verse 18 — NIV). His 'hope' was rooted in a miracle-working God and his promise.

It was not that Abraham avoided thinking about his own old age and his wife's infertility: 'He did not weaken in faith when he considered his own body, which was already as good as dead (for he was about a hundred years old), or when he considered the barrenness of Sarah's womb' (verse 19). Yet his faith grew strong only as he thought about God. He gave glory to God (verse 20).

Faith can transcend reason — it can lead us into regions which reason cannot reach — but there is nothing unreasonable about it. Brendon Byrne makes the point that Abraham's giving glory to God 'suggests that his faith, which has to be faith precisely in God as Creator, constitutes the explicit reversal of that basic pattern of sin.'[3] The contrast to this is chapter 1, verses 19 to 23 where the Roman pagans, Paul says, 'did not honour him as God or give thanks to him'.

(b) Isaac's last-minute reprieve

The sparing of the life of Abraham's son Isaac was understood as a restoration to life. Abraham reasoned that God could raise the dead. Figuratively speaking, he did receive Isaac back from death' (Hebrews 11, verse 19).

This line of thinking may be part of the background to Paul's conviction about God's power to bring life to the dead. Undoubtedly, Paul has in mind the raising of Jesus, as the last two verses of the chapter make clear (verses 24 and 25).

God is a God who creates 'ex nihilo', out of nothing. He 'calls into existence the things that do not exist' (verse 17b). The nonexistent capacity of Sarah's womb was the very place to prove God's ability to make the barren capable of gestation.

Both these attributes of God — his power to give life to the dead and his power to bring into being the 'things which are not' (NIV) — were in the forefront of Abraham's mind when he put his trust in God. God's power is made visible in creation out of nothing (chapter 1, verse 20) and in resurrection out of death. Abraham linked his knowledge of this particular God with the difficulties that stood in his way and in the situation threw in his lot with God.

The second century lawyer-turned-theologian, Tertullian, once said: 'I believe it because it is absurd.' Abraham's faith may appear to fit such a sentiment — a kind of leap in the dark. But unfortunately that is not faith: it is plain foolhardiness.

Abraham did not close his eyes to the facts of life which surrounded him. His faith grew strong because, knowing the facts, he still thought about God — his power and his will to do what he had promised. His mind was on true reality, God, and that was faith.

True faith has a specific object (verses 23 to 25)

The object of the believer's faith today is not only the God of Abraham, but also the 'God and Father of our Lord Jesus Christ'. Although Abraham lived before Christ, his faith had already (so to speak) the right shape, for Christian faith is precisely faith in the one who died (predictably), but then rose (most surprisingly).

In a sense, we are in the same position as Abraham towards the risen Lord. He didn't see him. We haven't seen him. He believed that God could raise the dead and would. We believe that God could raise the dead and did. We have the same faith. Those before and after the events of the death and resurrection of Jesus have to share the same-shaped faith because neither can 'see' these things.

The death and resurrection of Jesus Christ is seen by Paul as the hinge around which all history turns and therefore the hinge around which all 'stories' turn, including the story of Abraham.

Bishop Michael Marshall draws an analogy from the contemporary obsession with soap operas on television:

> Apparently meaningless lives, lived in obscurity and without recognition, begin to take on significance and meaning as the viewer identifies

with the heroes of the soap opera. Suddenly their love and their tragedies 'pick up' and resonate with the drama of the soap opera. The Bible is littered from cover to cover with theological soap operas, in which the central characters have a 'Jesus-shaped' profile to their lives and biographies. . . The 'opera' culminates in Jesus — in his passion, death and reversal to life.'[4]

Abraham was a 'Jesus-shaped' man of history.

Discussion questions

Talking it through

1 Religious people sometimes pride themselves on their humility. Is this a contradiction in terms? What are some contemporary examples of religious pride?

2 It seems difficult to accept that no-one is justified by their actions, and yet it is true. If salvation by good works wasn't good enough for Abraham and David, it isn't good enough for us. How can the following be a substitute for a living faith?
(a) Baptism
(b) Prayer
(c) Donations to worthy causes
(d) Acts of kindness or thoughtfulness
How can they become part of a vital faith?

3 How is faith more than:
(a) acknowledging the existence of God?
(b) feeling desperate from being unable to handle life by ourselves?
(c) clinging to God from a sense of inadequacy?
What is the content of faith?

4 If faith is not a leap in the dark, what is it? What is the difference between a belief system that contradicts reason and one that transcends it?

5 What is the cornerstone of Christian belief? What kind of evidence is the Christian faith built on?

6 Have you ever had an experience when God was particularly real to you? If so, can you describe it?

Widening our horizons

1 How is legitimate pride (in hard-won achievement at a personal or national level) different from false pride? How can justifiable feelings of pride, for example a sense of patriotism at our sportsmen and sportswomen succeeding at the Olympic or Commonwealth Games, become ugly, nationalistic bragging?

2 Think of the following life-situations:

(a) You are sacked for no apparent reason.

(b) You are accused of embezzlement or fraud, a charge that has no basis in truth.

(c) A bushfire or hurricane destroys your property and your insurance does not cover your loss.

How do you reconcile your sense of injustice and outrage with God's command to forgive?

3 The author argues that God's relationship with us fits the 'promise-trust' model, not 'employment-reward' one (page 110).

What is the contractual basis of the following human relationships?

(a) Parent-child
(b) Husband-wife
(c) Solicitor-client
(d) Shareholder-sharebroker
(e) Donor-indebted country

What light do these throw on our relationship to God?

4 Here are some common forms of advice to people in trouble. How like true faith is each?

(a) 'Snap out of it!'
(b) 'Keep your pecker up!'
(c) 'Don't let it get you down!'
(d) 'She'll be right!'
(e) 'Life wasn't meant to be easy.'

5 Consider the following people's lives. Which have a 'J-shaped' profile to them?

(a) Francis of Assissi
(b) Abraham Lincoln
(c) Leon Tolstoy
(d) Dag Hammarskjold
(e) Desmond Tutu
(f) You, the reader!

5
Our justification

What happens when
we are put right with God?
ROMANS CHAPTER 5, VERSE 1 TO
CHAPTER 6, VERSE 23

THE FIRST PART OF PAUL'S THESIS is complete. We are accepted by God, forgiven and counted righteous — justified — in his sight as a vastly unmerited gift. Paul now begins his next great argument, based on chapter 1, verse 17: those who are righteous by faith 'will live'.

In his love, God takes us as we are, yet he does not leave us as we are. His love is creative, able to make us more than we are or could ever hope to be. From Romans chapter 5 to the end of chapter 8, Paul will discuss what it means to 'live'.

It is helpful to remember that there are two Greek

words that are translated into English as 'life'. The Greek word *bios* corresponds to mere biological existence, the fact that we are alive and exist upon planet Earth. The Greek word *zoe* is used to mean 'life in all its fullness' or 'the full and authentic existence' that transcends mere biological existence. This is the mode of existence which has become available to us through the death and resurrection of Jesus Christ.

Paul proceeds in the following chapters to tell us something about *zoe*:

* It is a life which can rejoice in the midst of suffering because of an underlying 'peace with God' (chapter 5).
* It is a brand new 'muscular' faith which goes flat out to make a person as holy as it is possible for any sinner to be (chapters 6 and 7).
* It is a life which believers could never attain for themselves apart from the gift of the Holy Spirit (chapter 8).

To be authentically human means to be awake, curious, passionate and questing, never satisfied with things as they appear. It means, above all, to be free. And yet thrilling though the present life of a justified sinner is, this is merely a foretaste of what is yet to come. Paul announces a springtime of which all springtimes speak.

We have peace with God (verses 1 and 2)

The direct result of being in a right relationship with God — justified by faith — is that we have peace with God.

At this point we need to be aware of a vital distinction in Paul's writings. At times he refers to peace *with* God, as in our passage. At other times he uses the phrase 'the peace *of* God', as in Philippians 4, verses 7 and 11. Both ideas are related, but should not be confused.

* 'Peace with God' refers to that restored relationship which has been made possible through the death of Jesus, referred to in verses 6 to 11. It is not an emotional state of religious euphoria.
* The 'peace of God' is a state of mind which is free from anxiety.

Christian people do not always enjoy a peaceful kind of feeling about life. In fact, some Christians struggle with depression which may be brought about for a wide variety of reasons. For instance, *hypoglycemia* — low blood sugar — may be one factor which acts as a catalyst in bringing on emotional distress. And there are likely to be other factors.

The important point, however, is to see that because at any one time I may lack the peace of God, it does not follow that I cannot be at peace *with* God

— that I cannot be a Christian. A great deal of harm can be done to people struggling with depression by a failure to observe Paul's distinction here.

Peace with God is another outcome of the cross. As if using pieces in a jigsaw puzzle, Paul uses different images to build up a picture of what Jesus' death achieved. Peace with God, so important in this chapter, is one of these. God has taken the initiative in restoring our ruined relationship. By breaking sin's stranglehold upon us, he removes the cause of our alienation.

Paul will return to the theme of the cross again in verses 6 to 11. Meanwhile, he turns to the positive meaning of peace with God. Essentially it means *access*: 'we have gained access to this grace in which we stand' (verse 2).

The Greek word that is translated 'access' was used of somebody who was brought into the presence of a superior of some kind. It was used, for example, of subjects who were granted an audience with their sovereign. Today, we might talk about a professional lobbyist 'having access' to a cabinet member: he is able to use his political connections to gain a sympathetic hearing for a particular interest group. Or a salesman knowing the girl on the switch and therefore 'having access' to the key decision-maker.

Access is important in all areas of life. None of us likes to be fobbed off by some junior office clerk or receptionist when we are trying to get through to the manager.

'Justification' means that we have obtained access to the King of kings. God's declaration of us as righteous has important consequences. It's not simply an event that belongs to the distant past. It carries with it the immense privilege of being brought into the Father's presence. We are his guests.

And the access we have is not a fleeting access on the odd occasion. In this grace we *stand*: it is our permanent position, for we live in the presence of God. We do not fall 'in' and 'out' of grace. If we did, we would have to keep on being re-justified again and again.

Think of a human family. When we fail we provoke our parents' displeasure, but we are not therefore thrown out of the family. In the same way, the Christian who has been justified and adopted into God's family might grieve the Father by sin, but he or she does not cut the family ties because of this. Fellowship with God has been clouded, but the underlying relationship remains intact.

The Christian lives before God in a state of grace, constantly abiding in his presence. God *never* rejects those whom he has accepted.

We can handle suffering (verses 3 and 4)

But this access does not end all problems. Jesus

himself had constant access to his Father, but had to face opposition and scorn, injustice and betrayal. So, too, Christians must face suffering. And they do so with joy.

The stoic sufferer tackles suffering by gritting his teeth and bearing it. The stoic has nothing more to say than: 'That's life — a mixture of good and evil. That's the way the cookie crumbles.' But the Christian *rejoices* in suffering because it is seen to be part of a divine process.

It's not a matter of psychologically blocking out unpleasantness and shouting, 'Praise the Lord!' Believers rejoice because they know what is going on. God is making them into what he intends them to be: 'suffering produces endurance, and endurance produces character, and character produces hope' (verses 3b and 4). Or, to put it another way:

Watch his methods, watch his ways —
how he ruthlessly perfects,
whom he royally elects,
how he hammers him and hurts him
and with mighty blows converts him
into trial shapes of clay which only he
  understands,
while his tortured heart is crying
  and he lifts beseeching hands. . .

So the Christian rejoices not only in the end of this divine process, glory (verse 2b), but in the *means* to the end, suffering (verse 3). Clearly, this joy is to be distinguished from, for example, the fun of partying, the excitement of travel or the pleasure of achievement. We may have all of these, but still lack the solid joy of Christian experience.

Karl Barth, the twentieth century Swiss theologian, has described the believer's joy as a 'defiant, nevertheless joy'. We may be under pressure to the point of bursting — *nevertheless* we rejoice!

We have hope (verses 5 to 11)

The last link in the process of character-building is 'character [that produces] hope'. Those who work with the terminally ill know the importance of helping the patient work through to a realistic hope.

At first, they hope nothing is wrong. When they reluctantly agree to see the doctor, they hope it is not serious and they retain this hope as long as sufficient information is withheld from them. When that hope perishes, they hope something can be done. Medically speaking, they may end up being told there is 'no hope'.

The Christian therapist will then sensitively remind them that there is hope even if death cannot be avoided. As one preacher put it: 'the world dares say no more. . . than *dum spiro spero* (while I breathe my last breath, I hope); but the children of God can add by virtue of this living hope *dum exspiro spero* (when I stop breathing I have hope).'

Such a hope is formed, broken down and re-formed as a realistic assessment is made of the particular situation. It is not wishful thinking or unfounded optimism. It is a hope which will not disappoint because it is based on the immovable foundation of God's love: 'God's love has been poured into our hearts through the Holy Spirit that has been given to us' (verses 5).

Note that Paul does not say that the *Holy Spirit* has been poured into our hearts (as in Acts 2, verse 17), but that *God's love* has been poured into our hearts (verse 5). We have been enabled to know and understand this by the gift of the Holy Spirit to us. It is not simply head knowledge ('biblical headtripping'), but heart knowledge — something known, as it were, at 'gut level'. As Louis Armstrong once said about Jazz: 'If I have to explain it to you, you ain't got it!' God's love is appreciated, experienced, *enjoyed* by the person who knows him.

Paul argues *from* experience, not *to* it. His hope was certain because he perceived that, through all his sufferings, God's love was forming him and that in fact God loved him more wisely and far-sightedly than he loved himself. God had 'our hope of sharing the glory of God' in view. Paul knew that God was in charge of his sufferings even when it didn't feel like it. He knew, with heart knowledge rather than head knowledge, that God loved him because the Holy Spirit had taught it to him.

But the Holy Spirit had also pointed Paul to the cross. This is the other reason for his confidence in God's love. It had been amazingly displayed at the cross and Paul's thinking and praying was always focussed there. His certainty did not rest on experience alone (though we must not overlook the importance of experience in this passage). His spiritual experience actually deepened as he contemplated the love of the Saviour for sinful humankind. In one unflattering term after another Paul describes those for whom Christ died as 'weak' or 'powerless' (verse 6), 'ungodly' (verse 6), 'sinners' (verse 8) and 'enemies' (verse 10).

What is special about God's *agape* love is that it embraces us despite our flaws. Whereas human love is drawn to what it finds attractive, the love of God finds natural affinity with what is unappealing and unattractive. There might well be circumstances in which a person would give his life for someone else — if someone is held in high regard, for example. Even then, such a sacrifice is uncommon. Yet, as verse 8 says, 'God proves his love for us in that while we still were sinners Christ died for us.'

God's love is unstintingly lavished on us. This is most clearly demonstrated on the cross. Experience and history were the grounds upon which Paul was assured of the love of God. To him, God's love was as solid and awesome as the mountain peaks peeping above the clouds. This in turn is why Paul's hope was not a dream; it could not disappoint. It was based on the rock of what is real and permanent.

Paul affirms the certainty of our hope with a 'much more' argument: 'Much more surely then, now that we have been justified by his blood, will we be saved through him from the wrath of God' (verse 9). Since God loved us so much that he sent Christ to die for us, then he certainly loves us enough, now that we are reconciled to him, to bring us safely home. As someone has put it:

> It is as though a famous violinist offered to teach a child who had no musical knowledge to play the instrument. The first stages of instruction would be painful and difficult, going through all the basics of music and enduring the initial tuneless attempts of the pupil. But once that stage is over, the rest is pure joy; and what teacher would abandon the job when the hardest part was over and the best yet to come?

As Paul says later in a verse which encapsulates the meaning of verses 10 and 11: 'those whom he justified he also glorified' (chapter 8, verse 30).

Christian hope will not prove to be a mockery. If God performed the more costly service (involving his Son's death) for his enemies, he will certainly perform the less costly service now that his former enemies are his friends. No wonder Paul dares to say, 'We rejoice in God'. God's love is a love that will never let us go. There are certainly clear grounds for hope.

We have life in Jesus (verses 12 to 21)

We have seen that the burden of chapter 5, verses 1 to 11 concerned the certainty of justification. Paul was intent upon making it clear that the 'hope of glory' was not a matter of wishful thinking. Now he turns his attention to the one person who has made all this possible — Jesus Christ, whom he compares and contrasts with Adam, 'a type of the one who was to come' (verse 14).

We find this typological approach to the interpretation of the Old Testament in other places in Paul's writings. For example in 1 Corinthians chapter 10, he refers to the Exodus events 'as examples [types] for us, so that we might not desire evil as they did' (verse 6). The Old Testament type not only corresponds to the New Testament reality; it also stands in antithesis to it.

Like Adam, Jesus is the representative head of the race; unlike Adam, who brought death, Jesus brings forgiveness and life. Jesus is the prophet like Moses but, unlike Moses' ministry of condemnation, the ministry of Jesus gives righteousness (2 Corinthians chapter 3).

Scholars speak of 'synthetic' and of 'antithetic'

typology to distinguish the way in which a type either corresponds to or differs from the reality of the new age begun in Christ.

Jesus' similarity to Adam

When we look at the 'synthetic' aspects of the Adam typology, we find that there is really only one point of likeness being drawn. Adam, a single person, influences the destiny of many; Christ, a single person, also influences the destiny of many. The *unity* of the many in the one forms the critical point of comparison between Adam and Christ.

When we enquire a little further and ask how it is that the one man Adam caused many to sin, we run into a storm-centre of controversy. Some have concluded that we sin by imitating Adam's sin; others that we were constituted sinners by Adam's transgression and have inherited a corrupt nature; still others that we were in some mysterious way co-sinners with Adam.

Paul's language, strange as it may appear, seems to suggest that we were all caught up in what Adam did: 'For just as by the one man's disobedience the many were made sinners. . .' (verse 19). Our position in Adam can be illustrated from the representative position of the general in an army. If the general is defeated, every one of his soldiers is defeated.

Doubtless, even when we think we have grasped

accurately what it is that Paul is saying about *how* we became sinners, we will be left with many questions in our minds. But these questions do not alter the situation. As Alister McGrath points out, there are a number of facts about human existence which we have to learn to accept, even if we don't understand why they are so in the first place. And this is so with sin:

> It's just the way things are and no amount of arguing about it is going to alter the situation. The important thing is how this situation may be altered, rather than quibbling about how it arose in the first place![1]

Yet what is a basic axiom of human life for Alister McGrath is a major stumbling-block for some contemporary preachers. Matthew Fox, an influential Catholic priest, regards the doctrine of 'original sin' as a 'wrong turning' in the history of Christian thought, laying the blame at the feet of St Augustine.

Contrary to this view, I believe the 'wrong turning' goes back to Paul — and indeed to Jesus who seems to have inferred the doctrine when he said: 'If you then, *who are evil*, know how to give good gifts to your children, how much more will the heavenly Father give the Holy Spirit to those who ask him!' (Luke 11, verse 13). I believe we are all constituted sinners, however it happened — even the kindest and sweetest!

Jesus' differences from Adam

The 'antithetic' aspects of the Adam typology are more important to Paul than the 'synthetic' aspect. There are more differences than similarities between Adam and Christ.

Paul begins in verse 12 to make an analogy between the two, but breaks off without completing the sentence, because he realises the comparison could be misunderstood. We must imagine brackets enclosing verses 13 to 17. The long-awaited ending of what Paul began to say in verse 12 does not appear until verse 18.

Paul interrupts the flow of his argument to drive home the dissimilarities between Adam and Christ. With the strong word *but* at the beginning of verse 15, it is as though he wants to say: 'Hold it! There are differences — but the gift is not like the trespass.'

There are two important differences between Jesus and Adam mentioned by Paul:

❑ *The circumstances of Adam's disobedience and Christ's obedience are different*

Adam started, as it were, with a clean sheet. Christ started with all the accumulated sins of the centuries. As verse 16b says: 'For the judgment following one trespass brought condemnation, but the free gift following many trespasses brings justification.'

To live a perfect, sinless life of entire obedience starting from where we start — as Jesus did — was surely very much more wonderful than to have commenced where Adam did.

❑ *The results of Adam's disobedience and Christ's obedience are different*

Adam's sin brought condemnation whereas Christ's obedience brought justification. And this was not simply a matter of recapturing in the garden of Gethsemane what was lost in the garden of Eden. Christ has done much more — in the positive sense — than Adam did in a negative sense. It is not simply that the reign of death is superseded by the reign of life. Paul in verse 17 shows that it is much more wonderful. Those who follow Jesus are actually said to reign *in life.*

We would expect Paul to say that the opposite of death reigning is life reigning. But he actually says that *believers* will reign in life. Someone has said that 'the slaves of death become kings'. God's grace is superlative in generosity. It does not just pay off our overdraft (so to speak); it makes us millionaires! Paul is stressing the abundance of God's provision as dramatically as he is able.

Julian of Norwich, the famous fourteenth century English mystic, had a vision in which the Adam 'typology' is used in a different way from Paul. But the meaning of her vision accords with Paul's thought and illustrates it from another angle.

She saw two figures in human form in a barren

desert: a lord and a servant. The lord, who represents God the Father, sends the servant on an errand. The servant rushes with breakneck haste, but soon falls into a hollow where he lies badly injured, unable to help himself. The interpretation of servant is given at two levels.

Julian first sees him as standing for Adam — that is, one man standing for all humankind. Having fallen into a hole, we're too distracted by our pains and bruises to be able to face the effort of turning our face to God. We cannot see that he is truly very close to us. We are alienated.

But overlaying the figure of Adam, Julian sees the second person of the Trinity, God the Son, in his humanity — the 'rightful Adam'. He restores us by becoming one with us in our humanity, taking our sin upon him on the cross. In Julian's graphic perspective 'when Adam fell, God's Son fell' — fell with Adam 'into the valley of the womb of the maiden to take on him all our woes'.

Life in Jesus and the law

Paul concludes Romans 5 with a reference to the law and its part in bringing out the full triumph of life in Jesus. Paul points out two features of the law that are important:

- *The law has an intermediate purpose in bringing about the increase of sin*

'The law was added so that the trespass might increase' (verse 20). C.E.B. Cranfield points out that there are three ways in which the law may be said to increase sin:

* *Sin increases in the sense of becoming clearer.* The law shows sin for what it is: 'through the law we become conscious of sin' (chapter 3, verse 20 — NIV).
* *Sin increases in the sense of becoming more sinful.* The law, by showing people that what they are doing is contrary to God's will, reveals disobedience as conscious and wilful. Sin is contempt of God's standard of right.
* *Sin increases in quantity.* The law actually foments more sin. It makes the offence abound. This point is taken up in chapter 7, verses 8 and 9.

❑ *The ultimate purpose of the law, however, is to show the superabundance of grace*

'But where sin increased, grace abounded all the more. . .' (verse 20). This can be seen most clearly in the history of the nation of Israel. The climax of Israel's sin is seen in the crucifixion of the Messiah, but precisely there at Calvary, when sin had done its worst, grace triumphed.

The benefits of justification with which this chapter began come to us 'through Jesus Christ our Lord' (verse 21). Believers enjoy great blessings because they are no longer tied to the old humanity initiated by Adam, but to the new humanity initiated by Christ.

Life in Jesus is for all

In Romans 1, verse 18 to chapter 3, verse 20, Paul discussed the *certainty and universality of condemnation.* In Romans 2, verse 3 he said: 'Do you imagine, whoever you are, that when you judge those who do such things and yet do them yourself, you will escape the judgment of God?' And then in Romans 3, verse 19: 'Now we know that whatever the law says, it speaks to those who are under the law, so that every mouth may be silenced, and the whole world may be held accountable to God.'

In chapter 5, Paul argues for the *certainty of justification* (verses 1 to 11) and the *universality of justification* (verses 12 to 21). Twelve times in verses 12 to 19 we have the word 'one'.

This particularism is universal in its significance. The one man, Jesus, died for all — not just for the small company of Christians then present. God sent his Son to save the world — not just a remnant of lost humankind. There is a *broadness* in the apparent narrowness of Paul's writing. This teaching creates an explosion of questions.

Are millions to suffer the judgment of God who never had a real opportunity to be saved? How should we relate to the 'religious' people we meet daily in the shops and at work who identify with religions other than Christianity? Where do they stand before God?

We feel threatened by religious pluralism because it seems to call into question our basic conviction that Jesus Christ is the 'second Adam', the one and only Saviour who died for the many.

There are several broad hints in Romans that God does have regard for faith even when it is forced to rely upon defective and incomplete information. In Romans 1, verses 19 and 20, Paul claimed that all people possess sufficient knowledge of God on the basis of which they are justly condemned if they reject it.

But the converse is also true: it is possible for them to renounce their sin and seek God, even if ignorant of Christ's provision, so that on the day of judgment the evidence of their conscience 'will accuse *or perhaps excuse* them' (chapter 2, verse 15). Paul does not subscribe to the close-minded attitude found amongst some Christians today.

On the basis of the general revelation in creation and in human nature, James Packer writes:

> We may safely say: (i) if any good pagan reached the point of throwing himself on his Maker's mercy for pardon, it was grace that brought him there; (ii) God will surely save anyone he brings thus far; (iii) anyone thus saved would learn in the next world that he was saved through Christ.[2]

These speculations, based as they are upon the hints which Paul gives in Romans, cannot be pressed into a fully-fledged doctrine of 'universalism' — the belief that all human beings without exception will be saved. If Paul meant that in chapter 5, he would have torn up the letter and begun again from scratch. The clue to the meaning of *all* in chapter 5, verses 12 to 21 is to be found in the context. (Verse 18 is especially important: 'Therefore just as one man's trespass led to condemnation for all, so one man's act of righteousness leads to justification and life for all.')

Chapter 5 stands flanked by the long section on justification by faith (chapter 3, verse 21 to chapter 4, verse 25) and the presentation of membership in the faith community by means of sharing in the death and resurrection of Christ (chapter 6). Almost from the beginning of his letter, Paul has been concerned to show that all people, Jew and Gentile alike, stand on the same level before God. In regard to justification, the Jew can claim no special advantage.

Chapter 4 in particular makes it clear that Abraham's true family is not just Jews according to the flesh, the possessors of circumcision and the law, but the worldwide community of the faithful. The distinction between Jew and Gentile has been abolished in Christ and, when Paul speaks of 'all' enjoying the blessing of the second Adam in chapter 5, verse 18, he does not mean 'all people individually', but 'Jews and Gentiles alike' — not *all without exception*, but *all without distinction*.

The context of the passage determines the correct line of interpretation. That this is Paul's meaning is further supported by the mention of a need to be open to God's grace in verse 17. It is not 'all' willy nilly, but 'those who *receive* the abundance of grace and of the free gift of righteousness through the one man, Jesus Christ'.

In Romans, then, there is a clue to the genuine concern about the future prospects of those who longed for a Saviour, but never heard of Christ during their lifetimes. It is a grotesque concept of God which pictures him as one who loves sinners and desires to save them, but merely tantalises them with truth about himself that can only result in their condemnation. Such a God would appear to *delight* in the death of the sinner.

God's purpose in revealing himself in creation (chapter 1, verses 18 and 19) and in the creation of humankind (chapter 2, verses 14 and 15) is surely that men and women might seek him and find him.

The supreme revelation in Christ is not the *sole* revelation of God. We are often slow to come to terms with John's statement that Jesus was the true light that enlightens everyone (John 1, verse 9). To follow Paul's hints is to remain open and positive towards people of other faiths.

It is a curious thing that theologians have been

happy to learn from non-Christian philosophers, but have been — for the most part — closed to the viewpoints of people of faith. As one writer puts it: 'Why do we look so hopefully to Plato and expect nothing from Buddha?' Christians are not universalists, but they are not exclusivists either.

If there is hope for the unevangelised millions in Paul's statements concerning general revelation, it remains a hope that is firmly centred in Christ. As James Packer comments: 'anyone thus saved would learn in the next world that he was saved through Christ.' Paul's writings will not allow us to yield an inch on the position that Jesus is the one and only mediator, and all — whether Jew or Gentile — must come to him and through him. The apostle holds in balance an exclusive loyalty to Christ with an *inclusive* appreciation of what God is doing outside Christianity. He is single-minded, but not narrow-minded.

We die to ourselves (chapter 6, verses 1 to 14)

In chapter 6, the apostle deals with the bogus logic which some may draw from his concluding remarks in chapter 5, verse 20b: 'where sin increased, grace abounded all the more'. Does this mean that the worse we get, the better God gets?

It seems that as the tide of sin increases, the lifeboat of grace will float higher and higher; that

God's unconditional daily acceptance means we can really 'sin it up'! Paul emphatically rejects such reasoning. His counter argument makes use of two illustrations: baptism and slavery. In verses 1 to 14, he looks at baptism.

Christians obviously can sin but, while there may be slips, they are uncharacteristic. Verse 2 is probably better translated, 'We died to sin; *why* should we live in it any longer?' rather than (as in the NIV) 'We died to sin; how *can* we live in it any longer?' or (as in the NRSV) 'How *can* we who died to sin go on living in it?'

Habitual sin in the Christian's life is not an impossibility. It is an *incongruity* — it shouldn't be there. James Packer makes this distinction:

> How can a student who's been expelled from school, or whose school has been closed down, continue attending there? How can an employee remain in a firm that has folded? How can a wife continue living with her deceased husband? In the same way how can we, whose former relationship to sin has been broken, still continue in it as we did before? We can't. We have died to sin and that makes it impossible for us to continue in it.[3]

Such apparently convincing parallels, however, overstate Paul's case. The Christian *can* indeed sin, as chapter 7 makes clear. The apostle's point is that sinning is out of character. It is a departure from the norm rather than regular practice, because a death and resurrection has taken place.

There are two different ways in which the New Testament portrays the death of Christ. First, *Christ died for us*. Chapter 5, verse 8 says: 'while we still were sinners Christ died for us.' He died painfully and publicly for us. In his death, he took our place. His death was by way of substitution.

This view is out of favour at present, but it is a persistent strand in the New Testament and underlies the heart of this letter. As we have seen in Romans 3, verses 21 to 26, Paul argues that God's justice has been revealed in the means whereby sin is forgiven. Substitution is implied.

Second, *we died with Christ*. Chapter 6, verse 8 says: 'But if we have died with Christ, we believe that we will also live with him.' We died painlessly and invisibly in solidarity with him. Although the idea of substitution is still present, the key concept is now *incorporation*. By faith, the Christian is 'plugged into' Christ's dying and rising. This is further suggested by the various compounds that use the preposition 'with': 'buried with him' (verse 4), 'crucified with him' (verse 6) and 'live with him' (verse 8).

The idea of incorporation is not an easy one to grasp. It is perhaps helpful to isolate the various meanings of dying and rising with Christ in this passage. Jesus proposes to take us 'with him' through death into resurrection in a four-stage operation:

❑ *Stage one: conversion*

Conversion may take place in a moment of time or over many months and years. However, when it happens, it results in a radical change — so much so, that the New Testament writers liken it to being 'born again' (John 3, verse 3), to the emergence of a 'new creation' (2 Corinthians 5, verse 17) or — as here — to a death and resurrection. At a fundamental level it refers to God's gracious decision to look on us, not as we are in our sinfulness and woundedness, but as we are in Christ.

A familiar communion hymn expresses this thought as a prayer:

> Look, Father, look on his anointed face,
> and only look on us as found in him.

That is what in fact God does at the time of conversion. It is not the only thing he does. John tells us that the inward, secret, invisible action of God within the human heart which sets off the process of conversion can be compared to conception. There is no life unless the father first plants the sperm. Similarly, there is no spiritual life unless God imparts it.

Paul tells us that this invisible action of God stems from his decision to regard Christ's death for our sins as our death and Christ's risen life as our life. God's intention is that we died to sin when Christ died (verse 2), just as our new life began when Christ was raised. Leenhardt expresses the dying aspect in this way:

> God willed that this death should be my own death; when I look at the cross, I see there the victim who represents me objectively; his death includes my own, his death is mine, it is my death which he dies. In the intention of God with regard to myself, I have died.[4]

❑ *Stage two: baptism*

Baptism probably occurred at or very soon after the conversion of many in New Testament times. An anthropologist would call it 'a rite of passage'. It signified the believer's exit, with Christ, from all the old relationships and entry into a new frame of relationships, attitudes and obligations.

There is a temptation today to tame the symbolism of baptism and turn it into a comforting piece of ceremonial. Leon Morris has pointed out that the symbolism has violent associations. The word 'baptise' was used in secular Greek of people being drowned or of ships being sunk. In Mark 10, verse 38, Jesus referred to his death as a baptism.

When the word is applied to Christian initiation, we shouldn't think of a nice little church service, a gentle 'tinkering' with people's way of life. Our dying and rising is to be understood in much more thoroughgoing terms. Christian baptism emphasises death. No-one who has understood what their baptism means can take for granted or, even worse, take advantage of the grace of God.

The Christian is a Passover person. We have been through the waters of baptism, drowned and raised through the tomb. Having died to sin in baptism, we should not be complacent about it.

Bishop Michael Marshall has 'an enthusiasm bordering on an obsession' for St Augustine. He writes as follows of Augustine's baptism:

> 'Do you turn to Christ?' Ambrose would have asked Augustine on the dawn of Easter Day, 25 April, AD 387. For a lifetime Augustine had been preparing for this moment — all else had led up to this turning point: unbelief, doubt, faith, study, suffering, fasting, prayer and yearning. And now as the sun was rising on Easter morning, Augustine — who had been facing the wrong way (facing towards the west and the darkness) and seeing the world from this point of view — turned from the night sky of the west to the light of the east and the dawn, saying: 'I turn to Christ'. He was then stripped and plunged under the waters of baptism, raised up

> and taken into the cathedral as a new Christian
> to partake of the heavenly food of the eucharist.
> He had, he believed, passed in that moment from
> darkness to light, for it had finally dawned upon
> him what life through death was really all about.
> He had, he believed, gone through the waters of
> baptism as surely as he had passed through the
> waters of his mother's womb and as surely as
> the ancient Israelites had passed through the Red
> Sea — he had been *through* it!
> He had, he believed, already passed from a life
> which was in fact a death, through a death
> which was to be for him life — and from that
> point onwards would love and serve the brethren
> as a Christian, a priest and finally as a bishop in
> the church of God and in the community of
> faith. In a word, he had been baptised.[5]

When Paul (verse 4) is referring to the conversion experience of believers or its sacramental enactment, he uses the past tense: 'we *were* therefore *buried* with him' (NIV); 'we *have been buried* with him by baptism into death' (NRSV). In the last two stages, he uses the present and future tenses respectively.

❑ *Stage three: living the baptismal life*

Someone has said that baptism is 'a once-in-a-lifetime experience that takes your whole life to complete'. The baptismal life is made up of constant 'deaths', large and small, followed by many 'resurrections'. The New Testament rarely, if ever, draws attention to the actual experience of baptism as a past event.

What Paul and the other New Testament writers are interested in is the present significance of baptism. They viewed it as a 'speaking sign' or 'visible word' which was fuel for their obedience. It is a life-shaper. Sinful behaviour was seen as a drastic denial of the meaning of baptism. The fact that believers were baptised was used as a lever to spur them on in the pattern of constant deaths and repeated resurrections.

The *death experiences* are the denials of self in which we consent to go God's way, whatever the pain and loss, rather than our own. 'Who could have believed,' cries one of French playwright Albert Camus' characters, 'that crime consists less in making others die, than in not dying oneself?'[6] Our whole journey to resurrection is a continual dying to sin and selfishness — and this involves every aspect of our lives.

When Paul speaks of 'the body of sin' in verse 6 he is not referring to our physical body; he means a person's total self, the human individual. 'Body' signifies the whole person.

In colloquial language there are traces of this usage, as when we speak of so many 'bods' (or bodies), meaning so many people. The 'body of sin', therefore, refers to the sinful self — our God-dishonouring, self-serving, sin-dominated disposition. That, says Paul, was brought to an end by our union with Christ in his death.

But the Christian life is not negative. In dying with Christ, the believer enters into newness of life. The *resurrection experiences* are the joy, calm and contentment which come through the testimony of a good conscience and the fresh energy being given to love and serve again.

❑ *Stage four: physical death and bodily resurrection*
Physical death is certain. The English poet, Gerard Manley Hopkins, said what we all know: that there is no way to keep at bay 'tombs and worms and tumbling to decay'. One may be the most blithe spirit, but one fine day one checks into the hospital never to check out again.

Heroes and comedians, saints and sinners all have the lid nailed down over them in the end. Then the struggle with sin ceases.

Believers will die to sin finally and irreversibly when they die physically and at Christ's coming will — equally, finally, irreversibly — be raised up to resurrection life. For them, it will be 'a plus instead of a minus, an increase instead of a decrease, a filling instead of any emptying, a birthday instead of a wake!' They *live* with Christ now, but they *will be* with Christ in a more wonderful way in the life to come.

Note the future tense in verse 8: 'we believe that

we will also live with him.'

The key to what Paul is saying about dying and rising is to be found in verse 11: 'consider yourselves dead to sin and alive to God in Christ Jesus.' This is the first exhortation to this point. For five-and-a-half chapters, Paul has laid down the great affirmations that undergird the Christian life. Only now does he introduce an imperative into his argument.

Doctrine is to be put into practice. Believers are to keep on regarding themselves as dead to sin and alive to God. They are to consider not only what they should be, but what by God's grace they already are.

The Christian life is a matter of living logically. An example of this is when we say, 'Be your age!' We mean: 'Act in accordance with the sort of person you really are.' This is not mere auto suggestion. As John Stott remarks:

> This is not the self-confident optimism of Norman Vincent Peale. Peale's way is to get us to pretend we are other than we are. Paul's way is to remind us what we truly are, because God has made us that way in Christ.[7]

Paul does not say that sin in the believer is dead. Instead, he says that believers are to count themselves dead to it. We are to let the truth of our dying and rising with Christ — understood in the four ways outlined above — grip our minds and mould our characters.

We make a free decision to be God's slaves (chapter 6, verses 15 to 23)

The question in verse 15 suggests a possible false inference which may be drawn from verse 14b: 'Should we sin because we are not under law but under grace?' If it's grace that saves, does it really matter how we live?

We must not shrug off Paul's question here, nor the question in verse 1, as if they had no application to the church today. Much of the lethargy within the church derives from the casual presumption that whether or not we do God's will, we are safe within the ambit of his grace.

* *'Keep sinning — grace will increase'*
  In response to the question in verse 1, Paul pointed to baptism. Through their union with Christ in baptism, believers have died to sin and are alive to God.
* *'Keep sinning – we're under grace'*
  In response to the question in verse 15, Paul now points to slavery. Through yielding ourselves as slaves to God, we are commited to obedience. In verses 1 to 14, conversion was likened to a death and resurrection. In verses 15 to 23, conversion is seen to involve surrender to God. Surrender

to God leads to a status of slavery and slavery involves obedience.

In the collection of essays entitled *Merton: By those who knew him best*, there is an incisive if indelicate quotation from Thomas Merton, the famous twentieth century monk. Referring to the three monastic vows, Merton says: '*Poverty* — that's a cinch. *Chastity* — well, that takes a little getting used to, but that's manageable. *Obedience* — that's the [expletive deleted].'[8]

The spectacular commands our attention always. Evangelist and Christian apologist, John Smith, highlights the need for emphasis on obedience, unspectacular as it may be, when he writes:

> We have been taught. . . two things: one true, the other heretical. The true thing is that everything is a result of God's grace. The heresy is that you can call yourself a Christian *simply because* you have a right doctrine about the atonement, the Person of Jesus, the Book and so forth.
> Biblically, a Christian isn't someone who believes the right bunch of forensic arguments, but someone who follows Jesus.[9]

In some respects, the metaphor of slavery is an inappropriate one. Paul knows that and will qualify the metaphor in chapter 8 by speaking of believers as adopted sons and daughters. Meanwhile, he uses the slave metaphor because it does convey an aspect of the believer's relationship with God which cannot be better expressed. Wrapped up in this picture are the ideas of total belongingness, total obligation, total commitment and total accountability.

Of course, Paul does not wish to convey any of the demeaning features of slavery. There is no thought of cruelty or humiliating treatment such as was commonplace in the first century. That is why he goes to some length in verse 19 to explain why he uses the metaphor at all: 'I am speaking in human terms because of your natural limitations.'

There is no question of anyone being free in the sense of having no master at all. It is, rather, a question of *whose* authority we are under: either sin (personified in this passage) which leads to death, or obedience which leads to righteousness. There is no third alternative. Those who imagine that they are free because they can do as they please are deluded. To do as one pleases is to live in slavery to self.

Rosamund, the young girl in Margaret Drabble's novel *The Millstone,* discovered this in her promiscuous adventures with Hamish, a university student. She recounts:

> We took rooms in hotels and spent nights in each other's colleges, partly for fun and partly because we liked each other's company. In those days, at that age, such things seemed possible and permis-

> sible: and, as I did them, I thought that I was creating love and the terms of love in my own way and in my own time.
> I did not realise the dreadful facts of life. I did not know that a pattern forms before we are aware of it, and that what we think we make becomes a rigid prison making us.[10]

Sin is addictive and the more it is indulged in, the less easy it is to resist.

Paul traces the beginning, development and end of both slaveries:

❑ *The beginning of each slavery*

In the prayer in verses 17 and 18, Paul praises God for what he has done in the lives of the Roman believers: 'But thanks be to God that you, having once been slaves to sin, have become obedient from the heart to the form of teaching to which you were entrusted, and that you, having been set free from sin, have become slaves to righteousness.' They used to be slaves to sin and that slavery began at birth.

From birth there is in each one of us a rough, fibrous root of self-centredness. But slavery to *God* began, when by grace — that is why Paul gives God the credit in his prayer — they obeyed the gospel and allowed its teaching to shape their lives.

Christian commitment is not blind. It is derived from something that is believed. As Paul said in verse 17: '. . .you wholeheartedly obeyed the form of teaching to which you were entrusted' (NIV).

This has important implications for evangelism. As educationalist Brian Hill says:

> I cannot be said to believe something which I actually know to be false or silly. I must suppose that my belief has some kind of plausibility; my mind must give consent. That is why forms of evangelism which try to stampede people (including children) into verbal profession of faith without engaging their reason fail to awaken commitment. At best, they can guarantee only parroted belief or conditioned conformity.[11]

❑ *The development of each slavery*

Neither slavery stands still. Each develops. In verse 19, Paul says: 'Just as you used to offer the parts of your body in slavery to impurity and to ever-increasing wickedness, so now offer them in slavery to righteousness leading to holiness' (NIV). Slavery to sin expresses itself in 'greater and greater iniquity'.

The first time a particular sin is committed, it brings great uneasiness and shame. The next time it is much easier to do and the time after that we are likely to be able to do it without a twinge of conscience. Slavery to sin is a snowballing process.

Sometimes we are unaware, until it is almost too late, that we have been drawn away from God and the things of God. We thought, perhaps, we had been standing still, surveying life from a morally neutral vantage point.

This truth is well expressed in an anonymous poem:

Back to the church of my fathers I went —
the years had been long,
seeking an accrual of faith
to make my spirit strong.

I looked about me and saw
humble devout folk there,
lifting transfigured faces up,
drawing strength from prayer.

But no fund of faith was there for me —
only emptiness and doubt;
for years I had put nothing in —
what could I hope to draw out?

Each slavery develops: neither stands still. In one we get steadily worse; in the other we begin to approximate more nearly to the likeness of Jesus. The degree to which we have progressed in this change will be marked by the degree to which we exhibit the Spirit's work in our life as outlined in Galatians 5, verse 22: love, joy, peace, patience, kindness, generosity, faithfulness, gentleness and self-control.

❑ *The end of each slavery*

Paul concludes the chapter by referring to the results of each slavery (verses 21 to 23).

There is a sense of equivalence about sin's payment. Sinners get what they have earned. On the other hand, there is a sense of bounty in God's gift of eternal life. Sinners do nothing to earn salvation.

C.S. Lewis contrasts the end point of both slaveries in this way:

> Look for yourself and you will find in the long run only hatred, loneliness, despair, rage, ruin and decay. But look for Christ and you will find him and, with him, everything else thrown in.[12]

'The Prayer of a Slave' was written by Malcolm Boyd:

> Well, I don't feel perfectly free. I don't feel free at all. I am captive to myself. I do what I want. I have it all my own way. There is no freedom at all for me in this, Jesus. Today I feel like a slave bound in chains and branded by a hot iron because I am captive to my own will and I don't give an honest damn about you or your will. You're over there where I'm keeping you, outside my real life. How can I go on being such a lousy hypocrite? Come over here, where I don't want you to come. Let me quit playing this blasphemous game of religion with you.

Jesus, help me to let you be yourself in my life — so that I may be myself.[13]

Discussion questions

Talking it through

1 Compare Romans 5, verses 6 to 11 with Philippians 4, verses 7 to 11. Why is it possible to have peace *with* God while not having the peace *of* God? Use a personal experience or those of someone you know to explain the difference.

2 What clues are we given in Romans 5, verses 3 to 5 to enable us to cope with suffering? Have you seen this process operating in your own life? Describe how.

3 How would you answer the person with this question: 'If someone believes in God to the best of his or her ability, won't God accept him or her?'

4 'Christians are not universalists, but they are not exclusivists either' (page 143). What do you think the author means by this?

5 How would you define conversion? In what ways is it like being released from slavery? Think of the dramatic conversion of a famous Christian leader.

6 Is sin ever an impossibility for the Christian? What, then, does it mean to say that sin is an 'incongruity' in the Christian's life (page 144)?

Widening our horizons

1 Think of how people who are depressed react to the concept that they are important . . . to their family, to their friends, to God. Why might this reaction be wrong? What should be the guiding principle controlling the relationship between our inner life and the world around us?

2 How can being aware of 'what is going on' (page 127) help us cope with suffering? Explain this in terms of the following concrete situations:

(a) the loss of a job, wealth or possessions
(b) the loss of someone dear to us
(c) unfair criticism or active persecution
(d) persistent health problems
(e) discouraging world news

3 In the Adam-Christ passage, we have a partial explanation for the origin of sin in the human race. How does this help us understand the origin of:

(a) terminal illness such as cancer?
(b) destructive natural phenomena such as

cyclones or earthquakes?
(c) coincidences?

4 Think of the concept 'all without distinction'/'all without exception'. How does this illuminate the concept of equal rights, for example:
(a) for each sex?
(b) for each race?
(c) for each class or economic group?

5 If you were speaking to a Muslim about Jesus, what key points would you seek to make (For reference, see a book that presents Jesus for someone from a Muslim background, such as *The Way of Jesus*, Bruce Farnham, Lion, 1986.)

6 Paul argues (chapter 6, verses 16 and 20) that we are all slaves to something, yet people talk constantly about being free.
Consider:
(a) the business tycoon, 'free' to succeed and exercise his power in a free-market economy
(b) the swinging single, 'free' to enter into (and leave) relationships without long-term commitment

(c) the teenager emerging from parental influence, 'free' to do his/her own thing.

How do you reconcile such personal options of free choice with Paul's notion of slavery?

6
Rules and regulations

Why can't the law bring us to God?
ROMANS CHAPTER 7, VERSES 1 TO 25

COLIN MORRIS, a British Methodist minister, has confessed that Paul's concern for 'law' turned him away from any serious interest in this epistle:

> I was a Jesus-man, straight down the line. And I possibly bore a subconscious grudge against Paul who seemed to have been the Galilean Carpenter's fanatical stage manager, transforming a way of life so unfettered as a soaring bird into an ordered, organised and juiceless religion.[1]

All this changed, he says, when he began to realise that Paul's letters were part of a two-way correspondence:

> We have some at least of Paul's letters to early churches; nowhere is there any record of the replies he received, though there are passages in some epistles which appear to have been inspired by queries addressed to him or charges made against him. But they have vanished without trace. Paul, unlike the modern church bureaucrat, did not leave behind him a legacy of endless filing cabinets. [2]

With what he calls 'sanctified imagination', Morris invented some of the letters written *to* Paul. The following example highlights the empathy Paul conveyed to his readers through the frank sharing of his own experience in Romans 7:

> **My dear Paul:**
> The significance of my pseudonym will not have escaped you. I am a very rich man and, every time one of the apostles expounds that parable of the Rich Man and Lazarus, I die a thousand deaths! And yet the extraordinary thing is that I found it possible either to keep the law to the letter or else find a way round it without it interfering with my luxurious life — good food, the best of everything and, as a bonus, a reputation for generosity towards the poor.
> I certainly didn't become a member of the Christian community in Rome out of strong convictions. It was my aged mother who, though naturally comfortably off, was a lonely

widow and was visited by Priscilla and Mary regularly (and not to solicit subscriptions but to give her companionship). She expressed the desire to share the worship and fellowship of the church, so naturally I took her along. The elders asked my advice about certain financial and land matters, so I just drifted in, as it were: a fat, jolly, rich Jew with, I confess, a tendency to sleep through the sermon.

But your very intimate, personal confession that you were always doing wrong when you desired to do right woke me up with a start! I, too, have the will to do good, but don't seem to be able to summon the power to achieve it.

Though I have a reputation for being easy-going and cheerful in my social life, my business competitors will tell you that I can be ruthless and drive hard bargains. So I live a double life and deep down my conscience torments me. And the law I was taught in the synagogue filled me with guilt and I dreaded the Last Day when I would have to face God's wrath. That was probably my secret motive for leaving the synagogue and meeting Christians, who seemed to be able to believe in a God who is a Father, not just in the sense that he is the Founder of our race, but who surrounds his children with loving care.

I dearly want to believe that, and I would give up my fortune and beg in the streets if I thought it could be so. Your words have given me a little hope. Though our material circumstances

have been so different, you and I seem to have travelled the same road. But whereas you have been able, through Christ, to subdue your lower nature, I am carnal through and through. What must I do to be saved?
I shall await anxiously your next exposition of the gospel to the Roman church.

Dives[3]

This fictional letter speaks of Paul's 'very intimate, personal confession' as though it were a matter of the past — perhaps in Paul's preconversion days. In the exposition which follows, I wish to argue that the confession using the past tense in verses 7 to 11 refers to Paul's preconversion experience and the present tense in verses 14 to 25 refers to his post-conversion experience.

There are some scholars who doubt that chapter 7 represents a 'personal confession' at all. They point out that when Paul writes, for example, in 1 Corinthians 13, 'If I speak in the tongues of men and angels, but have not love, I am a noisy gong or a clanging cymbal', he is not making a statement of personal application. The statement is general. Hence it is argued that the fact that Paul speaks in the first person in Romans 7, verses 7 to 25 by no means proves that he is relating personal experience.

It is, however, going too far to exclude an autobiographic element from the scope of these verses. Leon Morris does justice to both insights:

> It is best to see the apostle as identifying himself with the sinner. He is speaking from the standpoint of a convinced Christian and telling us from his own experience what happens to any sinner who is confronted with the law. [4]

The autobiographical element should not be minimised, but neither should the context and general trend of Paul's argument in the chapter be overlooked.

The apostle's primary concern is to correct some possible misunderstandings which could have arisen from what he has already said about law in chapter 6, verses 14 and 15. There he said, without further qualification, that believers are 'not under law'. Does this mean that the law given to Moses simply goes by the board? Even if what is said in chapter 7, verses 7 to 13 reflects Paul's own experience (and it does), the main point of the passage in its context is the defence of the law, not personal confession.

Paul demonstrates both the law's holiness *and* its close relationship with sin:

❑ *The law is holy*

The law is described as 'spiritual', coming from God (verse 14); and 'holy', 'just' and 'good' (verse 12). These two positive statements should be given their full weight in estimating Paul's view of the law. He was no libertine. He regarded the law as God's gracious gift to humankind.

❑ *The law is connected with sin*
Though the law is 'by no means' sin, the fact remains that it is linked with sin. God has, in fact, used the law 'in order that sin might be shown to be sin' (verse 13). Paul develops, as we shall see, a threefold connection between sin and the law.

We need to be free of the law's legalism (verses 1 to 6)

The main thrust of the marriage illustration in verses 2 and 3 is to show that a death makes a decisive difference. The law concerning a relationship between husband and wife is binding only while both are alive. If either party dies, it ceases to operate. Death releases from the law governing the former relationship and sets a person free to marry again: 'if her husband dies, she is released from the law of marriage' (verse 2).

Notice, she is not released from the law *per se.* At this one point — as far as it binds her to a husband — she is free. A 'husband-type law' has no relevance for her.

Similarly, the believer through being plugged into Christ's death in baptism — 'we died in him' — is dead to all forms of legalism. The moral law is still binding — after all, it is God's gracious gift (verse 12) — but it will be observed as the result, not the cause of salvation. It is *legalism*, not the law, with which the believer is finished.

This death to such a legalistic approach results in a life of wholehearted, joyful service — 'fruit to God' (verse 4) — whereas previously the law served only to arouse sinful passions which were the pathway to death. Legalism and self-salvation are over for believers. They are set free to serve in the power of God's indwelling Spirit. This will be taken up and expanded in chapter 8.

It is important to be clear about the contrast that Paul draws in verse 6. We have already noted Paul's high estimation of the law as God's good gift. He cannot possibly be brushing it aside in this verse. Again, we see something of Paul's difficulty as he pioneers language to express his meaning.

The contrast is not between 'law' and 'Spirit', since in a few verses he is going to say that 'the law is spiritual' (verse 14). What Paul is contrasting is 'the old way of the written code' and 'the new way of the Spirit'. It is the law as misunderstood and misused which is to be left behind.

This is the sense in which we have been 'released' (NIV) or 'discharged from the law' (NRSV). But the actual moral law is to be established in the believer's heart by the Spirit — a point taken up later in chapter 8, verse 4. Paul is neither a legalist, nor someone who believes rules are of no consequence — a libertine.

We need to recognise our own personal culpability (verses 7 to 13)

The statement, 'our sinful passions, aroused by the law' (verse 5), seems to make the law responsible for our sins. Paul now goes on to defend the law from such unjust criticism. He describes a threefold relation between sin and the law in order to show that the real problem is not with the law, but with our fallen human nature:

❑ *The law reveals sin (verse 7)*

We may experience covetousness even though we do not know the tenth commandment, but knowing that commandment reveals our sin for what it is: a deliberate disobeying of God's holy will. Sin is dethroning God and enthroning self.

❑ *The law provokes sin (verse 8)*

It is possible that Genesis chapter 3 is at the back of Paul's mind in writing this verse. In the story of Adam and Eve in Genesis chapter 2, we see how God's prohibition (verse 17) was used by the serpent to bring about covetousness and, finally, death.

Leon Morris illustrates from the life of Mark Twain:

> This plain-spoken American said that most idealists overlooked one feature of the human make-up which is very prominent, namely plain

> mulishness or perverseness. Mark Twain said that if a mule thinks he knows what you want him to do, he will do just the opposite, and Twain admitted he was like that himself — often mean for the sake of meanness. But the fault lies not in the ideal, but in the man who reacts against it.[5]

Leon Morris adds the comment:

> Until the command not to do an evil thing comes, we may not feel much urge to do it, but when we hear the command our native mulishness takes over. But the fault is not in the command. It is in the mulishness in the sinner.[6]

❑ *The law condemns sin (verses 9 to 11)*
There was a time in his life when Paul imagined that he was observing the law and felt quite satisfied with his life. He thinks back to his days as a Pharisee. He was a happy man — living without any awareness of falling short of God's law. He was 'apart from the law' in the sense that he did not allow it to seriously question and convict him.

And then the full force of God's law came home to him. It showed up the seriousness of his sin. He could see himself as one who stood condemned before a holy God. The law rocked his cheerful illusion of innocence. It marked the end of self-confidence. He felt miserable — in fact, so miserable he could only say, 'I died'.

Notice the element of deceit in sin's method (verse 11). It allures us into both wrongdoing and the comforting conclusion that we are spiritually all right as we are. It tries to fog our minds on the issues of eternity. But the law unmasked sin's deceitfulness. When its full meaning impacted on Paul, he saw himself as one condemned by God — dead. Such are the devastating results of the law. It reveals sin, it provokes sin and it condemns sin.

'So,' Paul concludes, 'the law is holy, and the commandment is holy and just and good' (verse 12). It is 'holy' in that its origin and authority come from a holy God, it is 'just' or righteous in that it bears witness to God's righteousness, and it is 'good' in that it is for our benefit.

It is perhaps worth noting that there were three main strands of law in the Old Testament. Each strand finds its fulfilment in a different way.

The *moral* law, such as the Ten Commandments, continues in force for believers today. Jesus said to his disciples: 'If you love me, keep my commandments' (John 14, verse 15). The moral law is for our good. It has been said that 'law is to love what a track is to a train'. Just as all the propulsive power is in the train and none in the track, so all the power to realise the fulfilment of life is in love and none in the law, but the law serves as one necessary track along which love is able to push us to the end for which we were created.

The *ceremonial* law, concerning various sacrifices and ritual actions, has been fulfilled in Christ and has a continuing interpretative function in showing the seriousness with which God views sin and the necessity for the shedding of blood to make atonement. Since the death of Christ, however, it ceases to be part of the believer's obligation.

The *civil* law concerned the historic nation of Israel and is not applicable today.

It is helpful to keep these three strands of law in mind. Here the apostle is thinking of the moral law. Sometimes interpreters of Paul have lumped together sin and law as the 'tyrants' from which the gospel delivers us. Paul makes it clear that sin and law are not to be put in the same class. Of the relationship of the law to the Christian faith, the theologian G.E. Ladd has said:

> Christ has brought the law as a way of righteousness and as a ceremonial code to an end; but the law as the expression of the will of God is permanent; and the person indwelt by the Holy Spirit and thus energised by love is enabled to fulfil the law as people under the law never could.'[7]

In verse 13, Paul emphatically denies that the law is responsible for his spiritual death. All the way through this section the villain is sin.

We need to maintain our war against our sinful nature (verses 14 to 20)

Paul is still primarily concerned that no slur be cast on God's good gift of the law. Commentators have sometimes lost sight of this and become absorbed in the question as to whether chapter 7 applies to his preconversion or post-conversion experience. The issue is complex, but is really a side issue.

That is not to say it is unimportant. It is simply to keep in step with Paul's emphasis throughout the passage. Having said that, we notice two traits which point to verses 14 to 25 being a portrait of Christian experience, Paul's included:

(a) A change in the tense of the verbs

In verse 7 to 13, the verbs are in the past tense. As we have seen, this section makes good sense when it is viewed as the experience of all prior to conversion. Most people live decent lives imagining, like the rich young ruler in Luke 18, verse 21, that they have kept all the law's demands.

This is what Paul meant when he wrote, 'I was once alive apart from the law. . .' (verse 9). He really hadn't allowed the law to do its work in his life. It hadn't begun to humble him and bring him to his knees in repentance. But that is how all non-Christians live. Paul was no exception.

In verses 14 to 25, the tense of the verbs changes to the present and Paul depicts the position of all believers, including himself as an apostle, in relation to the law. Thus he says, using the present tense: 'I *am* unspiritual, sold as a slave to sin' (verse 14 — NIV).

Some find this too dark a picture to paint of the believer in spite of the present tense verb. It is important to see that Paul does not think that this is the whole truth about the Christian. We must not separate Romans chapter 7 from Romans chapter 8. As Leon Morris comments, 'It does not mean that [Paul] never does the right, but it is a strong expression for his inability to do the right as he would like to.'[8] This surely fits Christian experience.

(b) A change of situation

In verses 7 to 13, Paul describes how sin sprang to life through the law and finished him off: 'It killed off the happy sinner, for it showed him the seriousness, not so much of sin in general as of his own sin.'[9]

In verses 14 to 25, Paul describes his struggle to reduce the level of his own inner dividedness. He is engaged in a continuing conflict with sin. Verse 17 is not intended as an excuse, but as an acknowledgment of the extent to which sin, still resident in the Christian, usurps control: 'As it is, it is no longer I myself who do it, but it is sin living in me' (verse 20 — NIV). Believers have to endure living with imperfection, even though they want to be quit of it.

We need to live with both anguish and triumph (verses 21 to 25)

The logical consequence of what Paul is saying is this: 'I see in my members another law at war with the law of my mind' (verse 23). It is probable that the word 'law' here is being used metaphorically to refer to the authority and control of sin which makes Paul its prisoner. C.E.B. Cranfield comments:

> It is a forceful way of making the point that the power which sin has over us is a terrible travesty, a grotesque parody, of that authority over us which belongs by right to God's holy law. Sin's exercising such authority over us is a hideous usurpation of the prerogative of God's law.[10]

Yet Paul delights in God's law with his inner being (verse 22). He is not deprecating the place of the law. As a believer, he appreciates it in a deeper way than he had as a Jew.

The unbeliever's attitude to the law is given in chapter 8, verse 7: '. . .the mind that is set on the flesh is hostile to God; it does not submit to God's law — indeed it cannot.' By contrast, the law of God has been imprinted on Paul's mind. It is this mind which is being renewed by God's Spirit (chapter 12, verse 2) which delights in God's law.

There are two cries at the end of this chapter which come naturally to the person who knows God intimately:

❑ *The cry of anguish*

'Wretched man that I am! Who will rescue me from this body of death?' (verse 24). Paul's life seems so deplorable that he doubts if anyone could possibly rescue him.

Over and over again it is the Christian's experience to start each day saying, 'Lord, let it be all right today,' and end it admitting, 'Lord, forgive me for what went wrong today.' It seems to be part of God's plan that we are often left wrong-footed. We are not allowed to save ourselves, no matter how desperately we desire it.

But though this is a cry of anguish, it is not a cry of despair.

❑ *The cry of triumph*

'Thanks be to God through Jesus Christ our Lord!' (verse 25a). Paul confidently expects that God will deliver him out of 'this body of death' in the future. Already God by his Spirit gives partial deliverance from sin. Total deliverance will come at the end of time when we are set free from the conditions of life in the body as we know it.

Paul sums up what he has said about the double servitude to which Christians are prone. With this renewed mind, Paul desires to obey God's will. With his fallen nature, he continues to serve sin. However, continuing to serve sin does not necessarily mean lack of commitment. Christian commitment is sometimes betrayed by individual choices, but not destroyed by them.

As Brian Hill helpfully puts it:

> When we do what in our best moments we don't want to do. . . this is a lapse for which we need to seek forgiveness; it is not a reversal of commitment. It is no longer I myself who do it, says Paul, but it is sin living in me. In other words, my commitment is my willed tendency to affirm Christ in my life. I now regard this as the real me, and I regard my sins not as expressions of a contrary commitment, but as throw-backs to a 'me' I no longer believe in.[11]

In summary then, chapter 7, verses 7 to 25 emphasises that, whether we are unbelievers or believers, non-Christians or Christians, indwelling sin is our big problem and is responsible for the weakness of the law to help us. We now come to the solution.

Why is it important to keep Romans chapters 7 and 8 together?

Spiritual growth is not usually a linear progression. Those most authentically holy have always been most sensitive to the presence of evil in their pilgrimage. They often bewail the fact that, after many years of solid effort, they appear to be less advanced than at the beginning of their journey.

In chapter 7, Paul talks with relentless frankness of his own experience. As we have seen, some interpreters have felt that he must be speaking of his pre-conversion days when he writes: 'For I do not do the good I want, but the evil I do not want is what I do' (verse 19) and 'Wretched man that I am! Who will rescue me from this body of death?' (verse 24).

But this seems more the language of a mature believer; more than that, it is the language of an apostle. The person who has no faith has no awareness of the gravity of sin. In Psalm 36 verse 2, the Psalmist says: 'For they flatter themselves in their own eyes that their iniquity cannot be found out and hated.' But the Christian takes the vulnerability of being a disciple seriously. It is not always an enjoyable exercise. It means noting the self-regarding motives — self-asserting, self-advancing, self-justifying, self-gratifying — that fuel everyday actions.

It is impressive to notice Paul's clear-sighted realism. He does not see himself as one who has been given a special kind of sanctified disposition from which all inclination to sin has been removed. In many respects in revealing his heartfelt cry of anguish, he sets himself forward as the patron saint of losers. He admits to a very spotted form of virtue and it is this mark of realism which still has power to touch people today.

When David Watson, the well-known British preacher who later died of cancer, wrote his autobiography *You are my God,* a friend advised him not to publish it for ten years. Edward England from the publishers Hodder and Stoughton read the manuscript and commented:

> I saw at once why his friend, concerned only for David, wanted him to put the manuscript into cold storage. It had a degree of openness and honesty not normally found in Christian autobiography. Christian leaders proclaimed and wrote about the strengths and weakness of Bible characters — of Moses, David and the apostle Peter — but were less frank, and probably with good reason, when telling their own story. Honesty in autobiography is terribly hard to achieve and afterwards can be difficult to live with.[12]

Paul's recognition of his own continuing sinfulness was not an expression of neurotic self-hatred, nor the sick unrealism of neurosis. It was a healthy, Christian matter-of-factness. Father Michael Casey enlarges on what this involves in relation to prayer:

> When I am tempted, sin often results, although sometimes the outcome is delayed by a token resistance. This is the sordid reality of my life. My tendency in prayer is then to try to put my sin behind me. Acknowledging only that it was

> an interruption in our relationship, I want to forget it when I come before God.
> This is a mistake. It is like hiding one's symptoms from a physician. To go to prayer aware of the shabbiness of my life is a great blessing. I can approach God as the great healer of life's wounds, reveal myself in truth and receive help. If I avoid the issue by keeping up a barrage of words and holy thoughts, I end up exhausted and God is rendered powerless by my reluctance to be honest. My failures, I must learn, do not separate me from God.
> What causes the breach is an unwillingness to bring my failures into God's presence. The greater failure is not realising that God's attitude to my sin is pity, not blame.'[13]

But this is not the whole story. In chapter 8 there is a strong note of optimism as the apostle looks to the transforming work of the Holy Spirit. A sense of joy and freedom pervades the entire chapter. Both aspects of experience — the pain of imperfection *and* the joy of assurance, hope and spiritual progress — should be ours constantly.

Charles Cranfield sums up the relation of Romans 7 and 8 well when he writes:

> We are convinced that it is possible to do justice to the text of Paul and also to the facts of Christian living wherever they are to be observed only if we resolutely hold chapters 7 and 8

together, in spite of the obvious tension between them, and see in them not two successive stages but two different aspects, two contemporaneous realities, of the Christian life, both of which continue so long as the Christian is in the flesh.'[14]

In a word: chapter 8 is the continuing answer to the continuing problem of chapter 7.

Discussion questions

Talking it through

1 What point is there in having the imaginary letter written to Paul (pages 167 to 169) in our mind as we approach chapter 7?

2 How is observing the law the result, not the cause of salvation?

3 Why is sin so serious to God? Is it just God's private obsession, his problem?

4 Take one of the Ten Commandments. From your personal experience, show how a knowledge of this particular commandment does not guarantee it being obeyed. What emotions did such a failure produce in you? What most disappointed you?

5 What are some everyday as distinct from 'religious' reasons that cause people to fail morally: peer group pressure, the desire to be successful, greed, self-absorption, laziness?

6 When trying to justify habitual sin, Tony replied, 'Well, God is a forgiving God.' Is he? If so, does he forgive us if we continue to sin?

Widening our horizons

1 People can be technically correct in applying the letter of the law, but totally ignore its underlying intention the 'spirit of the law'. Consider the following everyday examples, all of them fertile ground for legalistic behaviour and attitudes:

(a) fulfilling the requirements of the Tax Office
(b) obeying family rules in the home
(c) repaying loans or keeping a promise
(d) giving to the needy
(e) giving a fair day's work for a fair day's pay
(f) being faithful to one's marriage partner
(g) driving safely on the roads

How can we keep these technically, but still break the spirit of the law? Are people who are legalistic in these areas of life likely to be legalistic in their relationship to God?

2 Think about the underlying cause of legalistic attitudes. Who are we trying to fool? Who are we trying to justify? Why is legalism so contrary to the gospel — God's extravagant gift of Christ to us, his boundless love of us, totally undeserved?

3 'People who are emotionally rigid are invariably theologically rigid.' True?
How can we remain true to our convictions without exhibiting the earmarks of inflexibility, intolerance and lack of graciousness?

4 The apostle Paul saw love and the law as complementary, not opposites. How does the law help define love? How can rules and guidelines be used, not negatively as a bludgeon or rod, but *creatively* as a goad or measuring stick?

5 Various historic religions and contemporary ideologies see humankind's central struggle or source of conflict differently. Think of the:
(a) Buddhist and enlightenment
(b) Marxist and the class struggle
(c) New Ager and self-awareness
(d) Sceptic and the power of reason
(e) Hedonist and the pursuit of pleasure
(f) Materialist and luxury
Where does the Christian experience his or her greatest struggle? Are there points of contact with any of the above?

7
Faith's reward

What is true freedom?

ROMANS CHAPTER 8, VERSES 1 TO 39

❦

WE HAVE SEEN THAT THE QUOTATION in chapter 1, verse 17 — 'the one who is righteous will live by faith'— suggested to Paul the overall structure of his argument in this letter.

In chapters 1 to 4, he explains what it means to be 'righteous-by-faith'. In chapters 5 to 8, he expounds what it really means 'to live'. God by his Spirit is able to do what the law (on account of sin) is unable to do: to give us life.

Apart from three brief references (chapter 1,verse 4, chapter 5, verse 5 and chapter 7, verse 6), this is the first time in Romans that the Holy Spirit comes into the apostle's discussion. Twenty-one times he uses the word *spirit* in this section, nineteen of which refer not to our spirit, but to the Holy Spirit. By contrast, in the preceding section, Paul, speaking in the first person, uses the words 'I', 'me' and 'my' some forty times. We could call chapter 8, 'Live in the Spirit'!

There is a great deal in this chapter about what Paul calls 'the freedom of the glory of the children of God' (verse 21). It is the Spirit who helps us to enter more fully into this 'glorious freedom'. As Paul wrote in 2 Corinthians 3, verse 17: 'Now the Lord is the Spirit, and where the Spirit of the Lord is, there is freedom.' Our liberty is hindered by all sorts of tyrannies. Chapter 8 isolates some of them and shows how we can begin to enjoy the Spirit's comprehensive ministry of liberation.

The Spirit and a liberating ministry go hand in hand. We are apt to tear them apart. In the words of Thomas Smail:

> On the one side are charismatic Christians who constantly seek the anointing of the Holy Spirit, but who have yet to show how willing they are to become involved in God's liberating activity in the world. On the other, there are social activist Christians who want to liberate the oppressed, without receiving the messianic Spirit, who alone will enable them to do so effectively. Oh for the day when the charismatics become the liberators and the liberators become charismatic, because Jesus was both![1]

The drift of Paul's logic in this chapter has been captured by a string of three negatives and a positive. For those united to Jesus by faith, there is:

no condemnation,
no separation,
no trepidation,
but expectation.[2]

All thirty-nine verses convey a profound sense of assurance and certainty because of the liberating and exhilarating ministry of God's Spirit. In the light of the teaching of this chapter, John Stott is right to claim that:

> . . .the Christian ought to be the freest person in the world. The fact that we are not liberated people often means that we have not grasped the gospel in its fulness.[3]

As chapter 8 unfurls, five aspects of the believer's freedom come into view:

Freedom from moral paralysis (verses 1 to 13)
Freedom to be a child of God (verses 14 to 17)
Freedom from the bondage of decay (verses 18 to 25)
Freedom from paralysis in prayer (verses 26, 27)
Freedom from the fear of disaster and despair (verses 28 to 39)

Freedom from moral paralysis (verses 1 to 13)

Christian freedom is defined in verse 2 as being set free from 'the law of sin and death'. Death is like a shadow, always following close on the heels of sin. Outside of faith in Christ, there is deadness — unresponsiveness in our relationship to God, both in knowledge and obedience: 'The sinful mind is hostile to God. It does not submit to God's law nor can it do so. Those controlled by the sinful nature cannot please God' (verses 7 and 8 — NIV).

By 'law' here, Paul is not thinking of the law of Moses given at Mount Sinai. He has already used 'law' in a metaphorical sense in chapter 7, verse 23 to refer to the authority or control exercised over people by sin. C.E.B. Cranfield suggests that Paul now uses it to denote 'the authority, control, constraint, exercised upon believers by the Holy Spirit'.[4]

Paul's teaching on various laws has been neatly summarised in this way: 'Moses' law has right but not might; sin's law has might but not right; the law of the Spirit has both right and might.'[5] It is the Spirit who begins to set us free from the dictates of the slave-driver, sin, so that we no longer come under condemnation in the sense of 'imprisonment' or 'servitude'.

We should note, in the light of the close connection between chapters 7 and 8, that the freedom spoken of here is not absolute. Absolute freedom from servitude to sin is a proud and dangerous illusion. Nevertheless, there is a very real difference between the attitude of the believer and the unbeliever towards sin.

The believer does not sit back and allow the tyrant sin to rule. When the Spirit of God is received at the point of conversion, the Christian's real struggle against sin and temptation *begin;* they do not end as many believers think. Yet there can be no grounds for pessimism. The control of the indwelling Spirit enables the believer to fight back against the power of sin with real effectiveness.

As James Packer has put it: 'Nobody has much heart for a fight he does not think he can win. To expect defeat is to ensure it.' And again: 'If I imagine that, try as I might, I am bound to fail, I shall not even try as I might.'[6] Paul's pastoral concern is that his readers become neither disillusioned nor discouraged.

The freedom to resist sin is expressed positively in verse 4. The whole purpose of the incarnation and atonement was to establish the law of God in our hearts so that we spontaneously desire what God requires — 'in order that the righteous requirement of the law might be fully met in us, who do not live according to the sinful nature, but according to the Spirit' (NIV). God's commands have now become God's enablings.

This transformation in attitude and ability is only

possible because of Christ. As Michael Casey says: 'He who was from all eternity "towards God" put on human nature in all its "awayness from God".'[7]

The NIV Bible wrongly translates 'just requirement' (verse 4) as a plural noun: 'righteous *requirements*'. The singular is used to show that God's law is not a collection of disjointed regulations, but a unity expressing the single will of the Father. The Christian is set free to call God 'Abba! Father!' (verse 15). When this happens with a full understanding of its significance, the just requirement of the law is fulfilled.

As C.E.B. Cranfield put it, calling on God as Father states in principle all of Christian ethics:

> . . .for there is nothing more required of us than that we should do just this — with full understanding of what it means, with full seriousness and with full sincerity. For to address the true God by the name of Father with full sincerity and seriousness will involve seeking wholeheartedly to be and think and say and do that which is pleasing to him and to avoid everything which displeases him.[8]

❑ *How Jesus has set us free*

The freedom to obey and begin to fulfil God's law is only possible because of what God has done in sending his Son. By way of the incarnation, he offered his life as an atonement for sin (verse 3).

The incarnation is implied by the phrase 'sending his own Son in the likeness of sinful flesh'.

John Stott explains Paul's careful wording in this way:

> Not 'in sinful flesh', because the flesh of Jesus was sinless. Not 'in the likeness of flesh', because the flesh of Jesus was real. But 'in the likeness of sinful flesh', because the flesh of Jesus was both sinless and real.[9]

This appears to be a reasonable explanation of Paul's phrase, but it may be that Paul's language is being stretched to the limit and the above explanation does not quite exhaust the reality Paul is seeking to describe. Everyone likes simple explanations and there is always a temptation to make Christianity as easy as it can possibly be. But there's a limit to how much you can simplify something which is already very complicated.

In taking upon himself the vestment of our humanity in the womb of the woman Mary, it would seem that Jesus did, in fact, assume a fallen human nature. But then Jesus transformed that unpromising material into a perfect human nature — by never yielding to the pressure of sin. He lived a sinless life.

Only in this way could he redeem what needed redemption — not Adam's unfallen nature, but our fallen human nature. As Professor Cranfield remarks:

> To live a perfect sinless life of entire obedience, starting from where *we* start, was surely much more wonderful than to have started where Adam started and managed not to fall. . .[10]

Yet though Jesus assumed our fallen human nature, he did not cease to be what he eternally is. It was probably this difference that led Paul to insert the word *likeness* in the phrase, 'in the likeness of sinful flesh'. He wished to safeguard the element of *otherness* in the human nature of Jesus.

Unlike our human nature, the human nature of Jesus was united to God personally. Paul didn't invent the idea of the incarnation. We see him here struggling for a form of words to capture its fullness and richness. In sending his Son, God did not don special protective clothing to avoid exposure to and contamination in a sin-ridden world. He *laid aside* his immunity to pain and temptation and came in the likeness of sinful flesh. As an Anglican communion prayer puts it: 'He shared our life in human form from the warmth of Mary's womb to the stillness of the grave.'[11]

Jesus' purpose in coming was to be a 'sin offering'. In this way he condemned sin in a sinful humanity. God in Christ bore the brunt of his own anger against sin, so bringing about an 'at-one-ment' (see chapter 3, verses 21 to 26). The freedom which the Holy Spirit works in our life was bought at great price. As John Stott reminds us:

> It is a wonderful and beautiful freedom and, when we prize it, it will keep us close to the cross, it will fill our hearts with gratitude and praise to God, it will move us to keep our conscience as clear as the noonday sun, because any sin which remains on our conscience, unacknowledged, unconfessed, unrepented and unforgiven, spoils our freedom as the children of God.[12]

❑ *How the Spirit sets us free*

Verses 5 to 13 are an explanation of the reference in verse 4 to those 'who do not live according to the sinful nature, but according to the Spirit' (NIV).

Paul sees the Christian as a walking 'civil war'. The old anti-God instincts and urges, though not dominant, are still resident. There is no equilibrium between these two forces. Powerful though sin still is over us, the power of the Spirit is far stronger and must triumph at the end. God intends us to become true images of his Son.

The Spirit is the 'saint-making' Spirit and he sculptures with a design in mind, Jesus: 'For those God foreknew he also predestined to be conformed to the likeness of his Son' (verse 29 — NIV). Thomas Smail brings out the creativity of the Spirit's transforming work:

> There are no stereotypes of sanctity. All the saints are gloriously various but, out of all the

> differing colours and textures of their created natures and personalities, the Spirit sets himself to paint a new *ikon* [image] of the Lord.[13]

The Spirit's way of setting us free from our all-pervasive egotism and transforming us into the likeness of Jesus is by means of *habit*. Positively, it is setting the mind on what the Spirit desires (verse 5); negatively, it is by putting to death the misdeeds of the body, the sinful behaviour patterns (verse 13).

There are many today who passively wait for the Spirit to change them in the twinkling of an eye. The Christian's motto, says James Packer, should not be 'Let go and let God', but 'Trust God and get going!'[14] Paul's reference to being 'led by the Spirit' (verse 14) is not a matter of waiting passively for celestial promptings and inward voices. In the context of chapter 8 it has to do with habit-forming: where we 'set our minds' and whether we 'put to death the misdeeds of the body'. It means a lifetime of unimpressive chipping away at the darkness within.

This is not self-sanctification by self-effort. It is simply a matter of fulfilling the conditions of the Spirit so that he can gradually transform us into the image of Jesus Christ. In the light of what Paul has to say in this section about the Spirit's method of working, we need to beware of quack practitioners of the soul who promise instant holiness by a given formula or a given experience.

Habits are all-important if we are to continue to enjoy 'the glorious freedom of the children of God'. Some Christians have what has been traditionally called 'a rule of life'. The idea sounds hopelessly legalistic to many ears. Perhaps it is better to think in terms of a 'pattern' of life, because this is what is intended.

This 'freeing timetable' will include time for those biblically prescribed habits which are the 'means of grace' through which the Spirit works — such as meeting for fellowship with other Christians, reflecting deeply on scripture and questioning one's own heart about what is read, taking time for private and public prayer.

In these and other ways we flesh out what Paul means by 'setting the mind on the Spirit' and 'putting to death the deeds of the body'. More and more we begin to experience the freedom from what Malcolm Muggeridge has called 'the dark little dungeon of our own ego'.

In this partial moral liberation, we have a clue as to what the Spirit will finally do for all who are united to Christ by faith: 'And if the Spirit of him who raised Jesus from the dead is living in you, he who raised Christ from the dead will also give life to your mortal bodies through his Spirit who lives in you' (verse 11 — NIV). *Complete* freedom from the presence and power of sin must await 'the redemption of our bodies' (verse 23), but then:

In a flash, at a trumpet crash
I am all at once what Christ is,
since he was what I am, and
This Jack, joke, poor potsherd,
patch, matchwood, immortal diamond,
Is immortal diamond.[15]

Freedom to be a child of God (verses 14 to 17)

Sometimes Paul has been brushed aside as a cold, unfeeling legalist, without the poet's heart or understanding of our relation to God. It is true, as we have seen, that Paul does use language drawn from the judiciary system to lay the foundations of the Christian life. 'Justification' is a fundamental concept to describe the beginning of the Christian life.

But important as that concept is, it does not exhaust all that is involved in our relationship with God. It is when we come to the concept of 'adoption' that we are made aware of warmth and security implied in a filial relation with God as Father: 'When we cry, "Abba! Father!" it is that very Spirit bearing witness with our spirit that we are children of God' (verses 15b and 16).

The distinction between the two concepts has been put this way: 'Justification is a *forensic* idea, conceived in terms of law and viewing God as judge. Adoption is a *family* idea, conceived in terms of love, and viewing God as father.'[16]

'Abba' is not Hebrew, the language of liturgy, but

Aramaic, the language of home and everyday life. It was heard on the lips of Jesus in the garden of Gethsemane, waiting for his betrayer in the dark shadow of the cross.

Theologian C.F.D. Moule has cautioned against the stock translation of 'Abba' as 'Daddy'. He says:

> Addressing his heavenly Father with exceptional intimacy, Jesus does not, however, take advantage of the familiarity. He uses the *Abba* address to offer to God his complete obedience. The intimate word conveys not a casual sort of familiarity, but the deepest, most trustful reverence.[17]

Probably the best translation of *Abba* is simply 'Father'.

Author James Jones has brought a freshness to this concept in a parable which is worth quoting in full:

> Imagine yourself a child, an orphan. In silent moments you long to have known your mother and father and wonder what they were like. You yearn to have loved them and to be loved by them. Although you are well cared for, you feel that you do not belong. You are rootless.
> One day, when on the downs, you stand watching a father and son playing together. They are laughing and enjoying not just the game, but

> each other. The love, the energy, the fun make you all the more melancholic. You ache for a father like that father and envy the son his place in the friendship of such warmth and affection. Here for the world to see is simple giving and receiving. While watching at a distance you wish secretly that you could join the game and so be caught up in the father's and the son's friendship.
>
> Quite suddenly and to your surprise the son turns to you and makes to throw the ball towards you, to draw you into the game. In that moment you are stunned. It is what you dreamed about. You are caught off guard. You feel embarrassed that they could read your need and your longing. How do you react? Do you turn away with embarrassment? Do you reach out to catch the ball. . .?
>
> The gospel story is about God the Father and God the Son drawing the world into their love. . . The Father delights in his Son; the Son delights in his Father. The love between them stands at the centre of the universe. The Father and his Son work by the Spirit to draw us orphaned onlookers into their love.[18]

The Spirit's ministry of assurance by which he draws us into the love of the Father and the Son is referred to in verses 14 to 17, but in fact it lies beneath the surface of every verse in chapter 8. We now look at the Spirit's work.

❑ *The way the Holy Spirit assures us we are God's children*

Most translations of verse 16 indicate that there are two distinct sources which witness to our assurance: our spirit and God's Spirit. So, for example, the NIV translates it: 'The Spirit himself testifies *with* our spirit that we are God's children.' But it is more likely that the verse should read; 'The Spirit himself testifies *to* our spirit that we are God's children.'

It is possible to draw an inference about ourselves from a Bible verse. In John 6, verse 47 we are told: 'Very truly, I tell you whoever believes has eternal life.' A person is able to follow the steps of the argument in this text and deduce that they have the gift of everlasting life. They can be assured of this fact, whether or not they feel any different.

Yet if the assurance is only on paper — even if it is the paper of the Bible! — there is something wrong. As Robert Horn notes: 'It is as though a newly-married couple merely look to their marriage certificate for assurance that "it has really happened". The document is vital, but it would be very odd indeed if they were not vibrantly alive to each other.'[19]

Over and above the intelligent and intellectual deduction of assurance, there is a direct and immediate assurance given by the Holy Spirit. Our human spirit plays no part in this. The context of these verses suggests that the essential nature of the

Spirit's assurance is to be thought of in terms of a deepening 'inner communion' rather than an 'inner explosion'. Theologian James Packer has written:

> The Spirit's witness is not ordinarily an experience in the sense in which orgasm, shock, bewilderment, being 'sent' by beauty in music or nature, or eating curry are experiences — datable, memorable, short-lived items in our flow of consciousness, standing out from what went before and what came afterwards.[20]

The Spirit leads us into a deeper experience of God as Father, not for the sake of experience, but for the sake of a deeper and more intimate union with him. His ministry of assurance takes the form not so much of a spine-chilling feeling as of a filial instinct and an abiding confidence.

❑ *The Holy Spirit's long-term involvement in assuring us*

There are moments of experience in which the Spirit's witness becomes suddenly strong. Michael Cassidy recounts a night in his life when all his senses were made vibrantly alive to God. He says: 'The Holy Spirit was blessing me. Wave upon wave, it seemed. Flow upon flow. He seemed to be bubbling up from within, surrounding from without, ascending from below and descending from above.'[21]

But the Spirit's witness is not always felt so vividly. There are times when it is overshadowed by feelings of doubt and despair. Our enjoyment of Christ may vary even though our union with him is secure. We may be tired and have a searing headache. That will not make us feel assured of anything! We may fondle sin in our hearts and become tentative in our faith. Many factors can affect our sense of assurance.

We are not converted because we feel converted, or lost simply because we feel unsure: 'We need not fear that the uneven quality of our Christian lives will rob us of our present standing in God's favour. It is heaven on earth to find oneself unable to doubt that this is so — and that is the essence of the God-given spirit of sonship.'[22]

The Spirit's assuring ministry is a continuous operation as is implied by the present tense verb of verse 16: 'it is that very Spirit *bearing witness* with our spirit that we are children of God.' This assurance — and the consequent freedom in the Holy Spirit — is not intended to be short-lived.

James Packer is probably correct in redefining what some Christians call the 'baptism in the Spirit' in terms of an *intensifying* of this ongoing ministry of assurance. It can be a very empowering and energising ministry. Nevertheless, we should normally enjoy a sense of security through the Spirit day-by-day assuring us that we are God's children. We should not willingly settle for less.

❑ *The victorious outcome of the Spirit's assurance*
When the Spirit bears witness to our spirits that we are children, he also assures us that we are heirs — heirs of the same One of whom we are children. Paul immediately gives content to this bold phrase ('heirs of God') with the further phrase, 'joint heirs' (NRSV) or 'co-heirs with Christ' (NIV).

To recognise this as our standing with God is not to succumb to an unthinking triumphalism; it is simply to state an objective fact. We *are* members of God's family and he wants to share with us his full inheritance as his legitimate children.

Everything that the Father gave to his one incarnate Son, he also has begun to give through him to his many adopted children. If we are 'joint heirs with Christ', we shall share fully in what *he* received. That includes glory through suffering. As Thomas Smail puts it:

> When in the Spirit we dare to cry *Abba*! after Jesus, the one on whom we call is the God of Gethsemane who can ask for anything, including ourselves, because he has given everything, including himself.[23]

But this suffering is not pointless or self-inflicted. The suffering along the way is for the sake of the glory and, in the end, this suffering will entirely yield to it — as has been done with Christ. It is by way of the cross, along the *via dolorosa,* that the triumphal procession moves.

We will not fall victim to a triumphalism that obscures the pain, but we will not lose sight of the victory either!

Freedom from the bondage of decay (verses 18 to 25)

The freedom to be enjoyed by the whole created order still lies in the future. We may begin to know freedom from the bondage of sin. We may also experience the assurance of being God's children.

And yet we have not attained, so far, what the apostle called the 'glorious freedom of the children of God' (verse 21b — NIV) or, as the phrase literally means, 'the liberty of the glory of the children of God'. Paul describes what lies ahead of us with two comparisons:

❑ *The groaning and glory of creation*

By 'creation' is meant the sum total of sub-human nature, both animate and inanimate. Before there was ever an ecological problem, God cursed the ground for humankind's sake, marring his own work so that it could not provide us with a heaven on earth: 'for the creation was subjected to futility, not of its own will but by the will of the one who subjected it. . .' (verse 20).

Animate creation is in bondage to the process of decay and cannot escape the cycle of birth, growth, death and decomposition. The 'thorns and thistles' which the earth brought forth after God cursed the ground (Genesis 3, verse 18) are a picture of nature 'red in tooth and claw'. As someone has put it, to become aware of the disruption of nature we only have to think of 'all the mice battered about and teased to death by our cats'![24]

Inanimate creation is also in bondage to the process of decay. Holes are appearing in the planet's ozone layer, pollution is being poured into the sea, larger and larger areas of the world have become desert, stars and galaxies are slowly running down as their energy dissipates itself.

Humanity's rape of the earth is a hideous and frightening story. The sub-human creation, both animal and vegetable, has been subjected to the frustration of not being able properly to fulfil its existence. In Paul's graphic language, it 'groans'. The reference here is to the labour pains of a woman expecting her child. It is a groaning that gives promise of the birth of a new order.

This whole section is poetic or, perhaps we should say, prophetic. Though the passage does not have the outward form of poetry in the sense or rhyme or rhythm, it does contain the inner essence of poetry.

The picturesque language of the creation waiting 'with eager longing' or 'in eager expectation' (verse 19) is reminiscent of the poetry of the Psalms which use similar personifications of nature: the 'mountains skipped like rams' (Psalm 114, verse 4); 'let the rivers clap their hands' (Psalm 98, verse 9). The creation is 'craning forward' — in J.B. Phillips' memorable phrase, 'waiting on tiptoe'.

Brendan Byrne says: 'It is almost as if nature is sensitive to something that human beings do not realise — rather like the stationmaster's dog, which can sense the proximity of a train long before the staff or passengers are aware of its approach.'[25] It is a longing for the state of affairs at the end of time when the torn fabric of heaven and earth will have been knit back together by redemption.

Whatever else this passage may imply, it clearly underlines the surpassing grandeur of what awaits us in the good plan of God.

❑ *The groaning and glory of the church*

Not only are animate and inanimate creation cheated of their fulfilment. Human beings, including Christians, are caught in the bondage to decay: 'Not only so, but we ourselves, who have the first fruits of the Spirit, groan inwardly as we wait eagerly for our adoption as sons. . .' (verse 23).

The apostle actually groaned audibly when he reflected on his bondage to sin: 'Wretched man that I am!' (chapter 7, verse 24). But there is a double corruption of the people of God: sin and *mortality*. We cannot escape just yet our bondage to decay, death and transitoriness to find the freedom we all look for.

What a dark vista stretches away in front of us when we turn to the plagues that bedevil our health: migraines, asthma, heart attack, hayfever, corns, cancer, stress-related illness! All of us lug about some sign of mortality.

But this present stage of life is not definitive: 'we wait eagerly for our adoption as sons, the redemption of our bodies' (verse 23 — NIV). We will be given a new body immune to germs and bacteria, so that there will be no more sickness or sorrow. Now we are 'parts outside parts', but then we will enjoy the total and simultaneous possession of complete life.

Cut off from the next life, Christianity is the ultimate foolishness. Paul's view of life stands against every perception of reality which is finite. He takes the doctrine of heaven seriously: 'I consider that the sufferings of this present time are not worth comparing with the glory about to be revealed to us' (verse 18).

> English preacher David Watson records the adjustment he had to make to his personal perspective as he struggled with cancer in these moving words: I had to make a very real transition from being willing to go to heaven but very much wanting to stay on earth, to actually wanting to go to heaven but willing to stay on earth.[26]

Notice the tension between the present experience of adoption in verses 14 and 16 and the future anticipation of adoption in verse 23. The clue to understanding this apparent contradiction is to be found in verse 19: we are *already* God's children. Through the Spirit, our adoption has taken place. But it is veiled and not always easy to discern who is and who is not a child of God.

The faces of commuters on the underground all look much the same! An open Bible might give a clue about the Christian identity of a particular traveller — but that is no certainty. C.S. Lewis, smoking his pipe and drinking his beer at an Oxford pub, might not look like a Christian to a South American Missionary Society convert in Peru. An Italian nun might have difficulty convincing the young student from the an evangelical student group that she is indeed 'born again'.

Faith is often scarcely recognisable across the lines that divide Christendom.

In the end, however, the true identity of the children of God will become plain for all to see: 'For the creation waits with eager longing for the revealing of the children of God' (verse 19). Heaven will be full of surprises.

Meanwhile, we live in an interim period. Behind faith lies the great 'no condemnation' of verse 1. Ahead of it lies the great 'not yet', the eager expectation of verse 19. Christ has come once and Christ will come again. However long the waiting takes, it is only 'the gap between the thunder and lightning'.

❑ *The willingness to wait for God's vindication*
This is the opposite of giving up the fight; it means persevering with the struggle to acquire virtue and being prepared for a long, hard engagement of the enemy. It could be called 'impatient patience'! By 'patience' is not meant complacency, laziness, resignation or mindless endurance. We should never be content with low and impoverished standards of Christian living.

'Faith's task,' someone once said, 'is to join hands with the past and the future to hold down God's will in the present.' This is possible because the believer has been given 'the first fruits of the Spirit' (verse 23) — a sample in advance of life in heaven.

In Leviticus 23, verses 10 and 11, the worshipper brought the first of the harvest to the temple and offered it to God. Here, instead of our offering God the first fruits, it is the other way around: God gives the believer 'the first fruits of the Spirit'! And the Spirit introduces us to the inmost essence of the life of heaven.

As James Packer puts it:

> What makes heaven to be heaven, and what must always be at the heart of our thoughts about heaven, is the actual relationship with the

> Father and the Son that is perfected there. It is of this that the Spirit's present ministry to us is the first instalment.[27]

While the Christian is in transit 'between times', there is a need for hope (verses 24 and 25). It would be difficult to find this need for hope expressed in better words than Tom Smail's:

> Hope has to do with God's promises that are still future and hidden, just as faith has to do with God's promises that are here and now. To the person who has believed for today but has not seen the answer come today, there comes the call to hope. Hope says, 'Tomorrow also is God's. Enough has happened already to assure you that the rest is on the way.' The first fruit promises and bespeaks the whole harvest.
> God is not by any means confined by today, as if when it is over all his possibilities are over with it; he is free to act tomorrow and, at any time, he chooses in all the series of tomorrows and, beyond that, in the great Tomorrow — when the whole inheritance is at last delivered and the sons of God at last come into their own.'[28]

Freedom from paralysis in prayer (verses 26 and 27)

When we fall to our knees in prayer, we do not suddenly cease to be needy sinners. Romans chapter 8 is still connected to Romans chapter 7! Our sin follows us even into the most holy precincts. It is encouraging to us lesser mortals, therefore, to know that for the apostle, prayer involves experiences of being at a loss either in what to pray for (content) or how to pray for it (method).

Weakness and incapacity in prayer has always been part of the experience of the great writers in the spiritual life. Theresa of Liseux spoke of prayer as 'the battle of the eyelids'. Father Michael Hollings talks about 'hours of dull, knee-aching, waste-of-time prayer'.

For Paul, the secret to being set free from paralysis in prayer was to view prayer as *gift* rather than duty. This is not to say that regular disciplined times of prayer are unnecessary. Prayer is much too important to be left to passing whims and moods. But we are to see prayer primarily as a gift given to us. In this way, the discipline becomes a much more hopeful and expectant exercise.

There are two advocates praying on our behalf: an advocate on high and an advocate within. We are *prayed for* by the ascended Son (verse 35) and we are *prayed in* by the indwelling Spirit (verses 26 and 27).

Part of our difficulty with prayer is that we think of ourselves as detached from God and having somehow to twist his arm to hear our requests. We see prayer as bridging the great divide between God and ourselves. We easily forget that it was Christ alone who has already done this. The result of that work is that we are now in Christ and he in us. Prayer becomes a participation in the conversation of heaven.

We are not the prayerless people we often take ourselves to be. As Andre Louf has said, the Spirit:

> . . .takes our heart in tow and turns it towards God. . . This state of prayer within us is something we always carry about with us, like a hidden treasure of which we are not consciously aware. Somewhere our heart is going full pelt, but we do not feel it. We are deaf to our praying heart.[29]

This chapter is full of reassurance. How comforting it is to know that, whether or not we pray another word, the Spirit of God is praying in us and Jesus our high priest is praying for us. Such knowledge is a lifeline of hope for any Christian struggling to wring some sort of prayer from a sluggish and often blank heart.

The inner logic of this passage requires us to use female imagery of the Spirit. Inarticulate groaning represents the birthpains of the new creation. We should probably translate the latter part of verse 26 as: 'We do not know how to pray as we ought, but the Spirit *herself* intercedes on our behalf with inarticulate groanings.' Female imagery is used for the creative and healing work of God *within* creation, just as male imagery is used for the work of the ascended Lord *in relation to* creation.

Freedom from the fear of disaster and despair (verses 28 to 39)

The freedom of the child of God is not freedom from disaster. It is freedom from the *fear* of disaster — and freedom from the bitterness, meaninglessness and despair which disaster sometimes brings.

God has made provision to set us free in all our weaknesses — whether moral (verses 1 to 13), mortal (verses 18 to 25) or spiritual (verses 26 and 27). He has also made provision to set us free from fear in all our circumstances. Paul knows that fear inhibits freedom and verses 28 and 29 will shrink and shrivel our fears as we meditate on them. These form the conclusion to chapter 8 and of the entire argument of the epistle to this point.

Verses 28 to 30 underline the certainty of that hope of which the previous verses have spoken. The apostle is a realist and he expects Murphy's Law at times to operate: 'anything that can go wrong will go wrong — and at the most awkward moment'. But he also knows that even the most disastrous events are not excluded from the action of God.

As the familiar saying goes: 'God writes straight on crooked lines.'[30] So Paul claims: 'And we know that in all things [including the pains and groans of verses 18 to 25] God works for the good [the true and ultimate good] of those who love him' (NIV).

Notice how the verse ends with a qualification: '. . .who have been called according to his purpose.' Our love for God is merely a sign and token of his prior love for us.

In his classic volume *Knowing God*, James Packer drew out the implications of Paul's qualification in this way:

> What matters supremely, therefore, is not in the last analysis the fact that I know God, but the larger fact which underlies it — the fact that *he knows me*. I am graven on the palms of his hands. I am never out of his mind. All my knowledge of him depends on his sustained initiative in knowing me. I know him because he first knew me and continues to know me. He knows me as a friend, one who loves me; and there is no moment when his eye is off me or his attention distracted from me, and no moment, therefore, when his care falters.[31]

Five affirmations (verses 28 to 30)

Verses 28 and 30 contain five great affirmations which give the grounds for the statement: 'We know that in all things God works for the ultimate good of those who love him.' We know this, says Paul, because God's plan for us is one that stretches back before time and on through history to eternity. Each link in this so-called golden chain underlines the security of the person who trusts God.

The security of the believer depends on the sovereignty of God. Many people today are extremely hostile to the biblical doctrine of election, as represented by the five links in this golden chain: *foreknown, predestined, called, justified* and *glorified*. To them, it smacks of favouritism and elitism. It is important if we are not to distort what Paul has to say that we set this passage in the overall context: adoption into God's family (verses 15 to 17).

Knowledge of election is the family secret of the children of God. An open secret, to be sure, but one which brings no comfort or benefit — because it has no application — until a person has come to faith in Christ (verse 1) and been adopted into God's family (verse 15).

The idea of God's selection of the elect and their separation from the rest is not in this passage. The state of those who are not believers in God is entirely absent from the passage.

Paul's intention is pastoral, not controversial. What he writes about is something to be enjoyed rather than argued about. It is knowledge which thrills, humbles and drives people to their knees to praise the God of their salvation as never before.

❑ *God foreknew*
Jeremiah 1, verse 5 says: 'Before I formed you in the womb I knew you.' We are not cloned to look alike or think and feel alike. God foreknew the unique self that each of us is.

❑ *God predestined*
Predestination is an incentive to holiness, not an excuse for sin. Jesus' likeness is the purpose of predestination. It is the ultimate 'good' for which all things work together: '. . .to be conformed to the image of his Son, in order that he might be the firstborn within a large family'.

An additional purpose of predestination involves the Christian community: '. . . that [Jesus] might be the firstborn within a large family'. The church is no afterthought. It is an essential part of God's plan and integral to the Christian message.

❑ *God called*
Here we enter the realm of historical time. Before that we were just an idea, a plan, but God's call comes to us. Maybe it is through a sermon, a sunset, a book or a conversation — but somehow God takes the initiative and we respond.

His call is always his *effective* call: it includes the idea of enabling a person called to respond. Paradoxically, what we do through God's help is more truly our own act than anything else we do.

❑ *God justified*

This refers to the favourable status we have before a righteous and holy God. It includes forgiveness and acceptance by God and has been at the heart of this letter's message. Paul omits any reference to the ongoing process of sanctification — being made holy. As we have seen, that is the purpose of predestination.

❑ *God glorified*

Our glorification lies in the future, yet Paul uses the past tense 'glorified'. Christ, in whose destiny our destiny is included, has already been glorified. In a sense, therefore, those who are united to Christ by faith may think of their glorification as having been already accomplished.

Earlier, the apostle referred to it as something concealed which has yet to be revealed: '. . .the sufferings of this present time are not worth comparing with the glory about to be revealed to us' (verse 18). The past tense is a most daring anticipation of faith. God will complete what he began. What began in eternity with his foreknowledge will end in eternity in glory.

Ultimate security (verses 31 to 39)

In the light of what has been said, not only in the last few verses but in the entire letter to this point,

Paul invites his readers to see the full force of his argument. All the themes from chapters 5 to 8 are brought before us in a few quick sentences. The object of it all is to make us certain beyond any doubt that, if we belong to Jesus Christ, then we are safe in the love of God for all eternity.

This is not an emotional fantasy. It's grounded not upon excessive confidence in ourselves or self-delusion, talking ourselves into believing we shall never fall or falter. Not at all. We are still under the weakness, ignorance and poverty mentioned in chapter 7, verses 14 to 25. It is founded on the 'steadfast love of the Lord which never ceases'.

Paul calls us to readjust our sights. We can too easily be swept off our feet and have an unbalanced vision of reality.

Bernard of Clairvaux, the twelfth century founder of the Cistercian Order, instructed his fellow monks to open the door of their minds to alternative thoughts:

> Turn aside from troubled and anxious reflection on your own progress and escape to the easier paths of remembering the good things which God has done. . . Sorrow for sin is a necessary thing, but it should not prevail all the time. It is necessary, rather, that happier recollections of the divine bounty should counter-balance it, lest the heart should become hardened through too much sadness and so perish through despair.[32]

There is plenty in life to be sad about, plenty to be anxious about, plenty even to be angry about. But the Christian is not a depressive. After all, just think, says Paul, 'If God is for us, who is against us?' (verse 31). If the God who foreknew, who predestined, who called, who justified and then glorified us — if *that* God is for us, 'who can be against us? (NIV).

Total up who and what stands against you and then remind yourself that one with that God is a majority. He is on our side.

Or again, Paul invites us to think through the implications of God's costly love: 'He who did not withhold his own Son, but gave him up for all of us, will he not with him also give us everything else?' (verse 32). Since God has lavished his love upon us by sending his Son to die for us, we may be fully confident: he will do what is, by comparison, far less.

The gift of Christ on Calvary guarantees that God will give us the fullness of his salvation: 'all things'. He will give us what is unimaginably the best.

The next two questions are addressed to those who are troubled in conscience. There are two sorts of sick consciences: those who are not aware enough of sin and those who are not aware enough of pardon. Paul has in mind the latter group and invites them to think through what justification means:

* Who shall bring any charge against God's elect? (verse 33) and
* Who is to condemn? (verse 34).

Many in the church today have a poor self-image. They are full of doubts because they think they are not good enough. They despise themselves and envy the successful Christians they imagine they see around them.

In justification, we know that God *accepts* us as we are, so who are we to reject ourselves? Even when we have sinned and rebelled and are consequently in no mood to pray, the ascended Lord does not cease to plead our cause and to intercede on our behalf (verse 34b).

It is in this confirming and effective work of Jesus Christ — interceding for us on the grounds of his great sacrifice — that we are taken to the heart of what Paul means by assurance. God accepts us. God will keep us. God holds nothing against us.

Paul Achtemeier has this encouraging point to make about verses 33 to 37:

> The only ones who have the power to accuse or condemn us — God or his Son — are in fact the very ones who protect us. . . whatever happens to us that we might construe as showing God's rejection — tribulation or anxiety, persecution or famine, poverty or war — has lost its power to mean that, because God is on our side.[33]

Finally, Paul asks: 'Who will separate us from the love of Christ?' (verse 35). Paul brings forward all the nightmarish situations he can think of which might be thought to separate us from Christ's love. He knows that frustration, injustice and random troubles, rather than any form of self-made contentment, are the appointed lot of God's people.

It has always been that way. Tribulations are nothing new. The apostle quotes from Psalm 44, verse 22 to show that suffering has been a characteristic of believers: 'For your sake we face death all day long; we are considered as sheep to be slaughtered' (NIV).

The English bishop, John Robinson, died after a long struggle with cancer. He echoed Paul's convictions when he wrote:

> God is to be found in the cancer as in everything else. If he is not, then he is not the God of the Psalmist who said, 'If I go down to hell, you are there also,' let alone of the Christian who knows God most deeply in the cross. And I have discovered this experience to be full of grace and truth.[34]

Furthermore, as Paul Achtemeier points out, to those of us who lack assurance and feel that we are our own worst enemy, even *we* can be overcome: 'If *no* creature can separate us from God's love, then in the end even our own limitless ability to rebel against God is overcome.'[35]

It was at the foot of the cross that Paul saw the love of Christ displayed. He does not say: 'In all these things we are more than conquerors through him who *loves* us.' He has a specific moment in mind. The past tense 'loved us' points to the historical event of Calvary. It was in reflecting on what God had done for him rather than in what he *was doing* in him that Paul came to such assurance.

Everyone who has lingered at the cross in thought and imagination believes in the love of God and everyone who believes in the love of God is free: free to live in God's love as God's child because he or she is free from all fear of disaster. Paul refuses to allow the questions he could not understand limit the joyous certainties he already knew.

There is every reason why Christian triumph must on no account be falsely optimistic, yet neither should a Christian, rightly rejecting 'triumphalism', be betrayed into singing the great victory hymns in a minor key: the evidence is strong enough for confidence. It does not, of course, amount to proof. How could anyone prove that nothing can stop God from loving us? The deepest realities of life are incapable of proof. Nevertheless, in the cross of Christ, Paul had strong grounds on which to rest his confidence.

He concludes with a word of personal testimony, using the first person singular, pointing out emphatically that nothing anywhere, here or hereafter, can ever cut us off from God's almighty love: 'This is my fixed, unshakable conviction. I am sure,' he wrote.

Paul must have longed for his readers to respond: 'So am I — hallelujah!'

Discussion questions

Talking it through

1 'The Christian has a greater struggle against sin and temptation than the non-Christian, but is more likely to succeed.' Do you agree with both parts of this statement?

2 What makes the Christian's struggle against sin worthwhile? Do you think the word 'sins' should replace 'sin'?

3 What is the Holy Spirit's work in our lives? What would we miss out on without him operating in us?

4 How is the realisation that God holds the future in his hands likely to affect the Christian's attitude to each of the following:

(a) success in business?

(b) the approaching death of someone close to us?

(c) constant physical pain?
(d) marriage?

5 Make up a diagram of what is happening when you pray. Include God the Father, Jesus, the Holy Spirit and yourself in the diagram. What understanding and encouragement can we gain from this?

6 You have the opportunity to provide comfort from Romans chapter 8 to someone suffering bereavement. What parts of the passage would you use and how would you use them?

7 What picture of God do you receive from verses 29 and 30? What sense of security can this provide you with?

8 What encouragement is given to each of the following from verses 29 and 30:
(a) those feeling hassled by the problems of life?
(b) those lacking confidence in God?
(c) those burdened down by a deep sense of guilt?

Widening our horizons

1 How would each of the following handle the problem of personal sin:

(a) a Christian ('God is the Lord of creation and of my life')?

(b) a deist ('a God-force is behind the universe')?

(c) a relativist ('nothing is absolute')?

Why would each take this particular view? Which view do you find most satisfying?

2 How did sin affect the lives of each of the following:

(a) Augustine?

(b) Jesus?

(c) Mahatma Gandhi?

(d) Paul?

3 What is the view of God that each of the following would be expected to have:

(a) a Christian?

(b) a Muslim?

(c) a Hindu?

(d) an animist?

How are these views reflected in relationships towards others?

4 What elements are present in each of the following human relationships that can also be present in our relationship with God:
(a) husband and wife?
(b) parent and child?
(c) parent and adopted child?
(d) ruler and subject?

5 What are good reasons why Christians could be involved in the following movements:
(a) preservation of natural forests?
(b) opposition to nuclear ships in our harbours?
(c) protection of Antarctica from commercial exploitation?
How might these reasons be different from those of non-Christian environmentalists? Could a Christian stand as a candidate for a green party?

6 What view of time is suggested by 'God foreknew', 'God predestined', 'God glorified'? Has a contemporary scientific understanding of space-time anything to contribute to such questions?

7 On a scale of descending reliability, rank the confidence you have about how long-lasting each of the following is:

(a) the love people have for those they love most
(b) God's love for us
(c) the universe going on much as it has
(d) your country being economically and politically stable

What can you conclude from this exercise? Is scientific 'proof' possible for any of these?

Endnotes

Introduction

1. M. Luther, 'Preface to the Epistle of St Paul to the Romans' in J. Dillenberger, *Martin Luther*, Anchor Books, 1961, p.19
2. J. Calvin, *Commentary on Romans*, Eerdmans, 1947, p.29
3. P. Achtemeier, *Romans*, John Knox, 1985
4. M. Harper, *Let my People Grow*, Hodder & Stoughton, 1977, p.12
5. L. Morris, in *Themelios*, Vol.8, No.1, September 1982, p.16
6. C.E.B. Cranfield, *A Critical and Exegetical Commentary on the Epistle to the Romans*, Vol.1, T.& T. Clark, 1975, p.40
7. L. Morris, *Glory in the Cross*, Hodder & Stoughton, 1966, p.33
8. W. Gasque, *Apostolic History and the Gospel*, Paternoster, 1970, pp.250 and 263
9. P. Achtemeier, *Romans*, John Knox, 1985, p.15
10. C.E.B. Cranfield, *A Critical and Exegetical Commentary on the Epistle to the Romans*, Vol.2, T.& T. Clark, 1979, p.853

11. S. Westerholm, *Israel's Law and the Church's Faith*, Eerdmans, 1988, p.132
12. R. Banks, *The Tyranny of Time*, Lancer, 1983, p.195

Chapter 1 – Paul the apostle

1. C.K. Barrett, *Reading through Romans*, Epworth, 1963, pp.10 and 11
2. R. Banks, *Interchange 30*, 1982, p.42
3. C. Sherlock, Review, in Christian Book Newsletter, Vol.4, No.2, April 1986, p.6
4. S.Travis, *I believe in the Second Coming of Jesus*, Hodder and Stoughton, 1982, p.132
5. J.I. Packer, *Knowing God*, Hodder and Stoughton, 1973, p.241
6. A. McGrath, *Justification by Faith*, Marshall Pickering, 1988, p.105

Chapter 2 – The human predicament

1. W.H. Willimon, *Sighing for Eden*, Abingdon, 1985, p.17
2. R.C. Sproul, *If There's a God, Why Are There Atheists?*, Tyndale House, 1988, p.57
3. S. Turner, 'Untitled', in Steve Turner, *Update*, Lion, 1982, p.22
4. Quoted from the leaked Osborne Report as published in *Church Times*, 16 February 1990
5. Letters to the Editor, *Church Times*, 2 March 1990
6. L. Pierson, *No-Gay Areas: Pastoral Care of Homosexual Christians*, Grove Pastoral Series No.38, Grove Books, 1989, p.13
7. Elizabeth Nance, *On Being*, December 1989 – January 1990, p.59
8. J.J. Packer, *Knowing God*, Hodder and Stoughton, 1973, p.130
9. J.V. Taylor, *The Go-between God*, SCM, 1972, p.172

10. D. Buchanan, *The Counselling of Jesus*, Hodder and Stoughton, 1985, p.91
11. M. Muggeridge, *Jesus Rediscovered*, Collins Fontana, 1969, p.32
12. D.S. Briscoe, *The Communicator's Commentary: Romans*, Word, 1982, p.77
13. R.M. Horn, *Go free!*, IVP, 1976, p.17

Chapter 3 – God's solution

1. A. Le Roy, 'Pastoral Counselling and self-justification', in *Journal of Psychology and Christianity* 3, No.4, Winter 1984, p.23
2. J. McIntyre, *On Being*, November 1985, p.27
3. P. Tournier, *Guilt and Grace*, Hodder and Stoughton, 1962, p.195
4. Augustine, *Confessions*, XLI 4, p.231
5. M. Goguel, *The Life of Jesus*, 1958, p.535
6. G.E. Ladd, *A Theology of the New Testament*, Lutterworth, 1974, p.441
7. L. Morris, *The Cross of Jesus*, Eerdmans, 1988, p.8

Chapter 4 – Genuine faith

1. D.S. Briscoe, *The Communicator's Commentary: Romans*, Word, 1982, p.101
2. L. Morris, *The Epistle to the Romans*, Eerdmans, 1988, p.213
3. B. Byrne, *Reckoning with Romans*, Glazier, 1986, p.101
4. M. Marshall, *A Change of Heart*, Collins, 1981, p.25

Chapter 5 – Our justification

1. Alister McGrath, *Justification by Faith*, Marshall Pickering, 1988, p.86

2. J. I. Packer, source unknown by author
3. J. Watson (ed.), *Through the year with J.I. Packer*, Hodder and Stoughton, 1986, p.319
4. L. Morris, *The Epistle to the Romans*, Eerdmans, p.247, footnote 16
5. M. Marshall, *A Change of Heart*, Collins, 1981, p.48
6. A. Camus, *The Fall*, Penguin, 1963, p.83
7. J. Stott, *Your Mind Matters*, IVP, 1972, p.34
8. P. Wilkes (ed.), *Merton: By Those Who Knew Him Best*, Harper & Row, 1984, p.89
9. J. Smith, 'Claims versus Pains', in *On Being*, July 1988, p.31
10. M. Drabble, *The Millstone*, Penguin, 1965, p.7
11. B. Hill, *The Greening of Christian Education*, Lancer, 1985, p.86
12. C.S. Lewis, *Mere Christianity*, Collins Fontana, 1952, p.188
13. M. Hollings, *The One Who Listens*, Hodder and Stoughton, 1971, p.136

Chapter 6 – Rules and regulations

1. C. Morris, *Epistles to the Apostle*, Hodder and Stoughton, p.10
2. *ibid*
3. *ibid*, p.117
4. L. Morris, *The Epistle to the Romans*, Eerdmans, p.277
5. *ibid*, p.280
6. *ibid*
7. G.E. Ladd, *A Theology of the New Testament*, Lutterworth, 1974, p.510
8. L. Morris, *The Epistle to the Romans*, Eerdmans, p.291
9. *ibid*, p.282
10. C.E.B. Cranfield, *Romans: A Shorter Commentary*, T.&T.

Clark, 1985, p.168

11. B. Hill, *The Greening of Christian Educaqtion*, Lancer, 1985, p.86
12. E. England, *David Watson: A Portrait by his Friends*, Hodder and Stoughton, 1985, p.163
13. M. Casey, *Towards God*, Collins Dove, 1989, p.153
14. Cranfield, *op.cit.*, p.164

Chapter 7 – Faith's reward

1. Thomas Smail, *The Giving Gift*, Hodder & Stoughton, 1988, p.104
2. J.I. Packer, *Keep in Step with the Spirit*, IVP, 1984, p.129
3. J. Stott, in *Southern Cross*, May 1980, p.26
4. C.E.B. Cranfield, *Romans: A Shorter Commentary*, T.&T. Clark, 1985, p.174
5. L. Morris, *The Epistle to the Romans*, Eerdmans, p.301
6. Packer, *op.cit.*
7. M. Casey, *Towards God*, Collins Dove, 1989, p.150
8. C.E.B. Cranfield, *op.cit.*, p.184
9. J. Stott, *Men Made New*, IVF, 1966, p.81
10. C.E.B. Cranfield, in correspondence to questioner. See further Cranfield's *A Critical and Exegetical Commentary on the Epistle to the Romans, Vol.1*, T.&T. Clark, 1975, p.383, note 2
11. *Patterns for Worship*, Church House Publishing, 1990, p.241
12. J. Stott, in a sermon preached in 1977 at All Soul's, Langham Place, London, entitled, 'Freedom from the condemnation of God'
13. Thomas Smail, *op.cit.*, p.180
14. J.I. Packer, *op.cit.*, p.157
15. G.M. Hopkins, 'That Nature is a Heraclitean Fire. . .' in W.H. Gardner (ed.), *Poems and Prose of Gerard Manley*

Hopkins, Penguin, 1958, p.65

16. J.I. Packer, *Knowing God*, Hodder and Stoughton, 1973, p.187
17. Thomas Smail, *The Forgotten Father*, Hodder and Stoughton, 1980, p.39
18. J. Jones, *Servant*, Darton, Longman and Todd, 1988, p.98
19. R.M. Horn, *Go free!*, IVP, 1976, p.79
20. J. Watson (ed.), *Through the year with J.I. Packer*, Hodder and Stoughton, 1986, p.19
21. M. Cassidy, *Bursting the Wineskins*, Hodder and Stoughton, 1983, p.122
22. J. Watson, *Through the Year with J.I. Packer*, Hodder and Stoughton, 1986, p.127
23. Thomas Smail, *op.cit.* p.37
24. T. Howard and J. Packer, *Christian Humanism*, Word, 1985, p.108
25. B. Byrne, *Reckoning with Romans*, Glazier, 1986, p.166
26. D. Watson, in a tape-recorded interview. See also his *Fear No Evil*, Hodder and Stoughton, 1984
27. J.I. Packer, *Keep in Step with the Spirit*, IVP, 1984, p.79
28. Thomas Smail, *The Forgotten Father*, Hodder & Stoughton, 1988, p.209
29. Thomas Smail, *The Giving Gift*, Hodder & Stoughton, 1988, p.209
30. Ecclesiastes 7, verse 13 is interesting in this respect.
31. J.I. Packer, *Knowing God*, Hodder and Stoughton, 1973, p.37
32. M. Casey, *A Thirst for God*, Cistercian Publications, 1987, p.306
33. P. Achtemeier, *Romans*, John Knox, 1985, p.149
34. J. Robinson, 'My God in My Cancer', in *The Age*, 16 December 1983
35. P. Achtemeier, *Romans*, John Knox, 1985, p.150

Bibliography

Useful commentaries on Romans

Paul Achtemeier, *Romans*, John Knox, 1985

A scholarly treatment of both the meaning and significance of the text.

C.K. Barrett, *A Commentary on the Epistle to the Romans*, Black, 1962

A helpful commentary which takes a pejorative view of law in Paul's thought, a point of divergence from Cranfield and this writer.

Karl Barth, *The Epistle to the Romans*, Oxford, 1933

A commentary by a widely respected scholar that provides a comprehensive and personal verse-by-verse treatment of the text.

F.F. Bruce, *Romans: An Introduction and Commentary*, IVP, 1969

Written by a widely acknowledged scholar, the special feature of this commentary is a detailed treatment of key words and expressions.

C.E.B. Cranfield, *Romans: A Shorter Commentary*, T.&T. Clark, 1985
A condensed version of Cranfield's two-volume commentary on the Greek text. The author looks at alternative interpretations of text, assesses them and provides modern applications.

Leon Morris, *The Epistle to the Romans*, Eerdmans, 1988
A commentary combining the best scholarship with helpful devotional insights. The significance of Jesus' death on the cross is never far from Paul's thoughts and Leon Morris mirrors the same emphasis in page after page.

J.A.T. Robinson, *Wrestling with Romans*, SCM, 1979
The author rightly claims to offer a 'conducted tour' through Romans, drawing attention to points of interest, helping through the difficult parts and bringing out the contemporary relevance.

Useful investigations of key ideas in Romans

Tony Baker, George Carey, John Tiller and Tom Wright, *The Great Acquittal*, Fount, 1980
A number of thought-provoking essays that relate the doctrine of justification by faith as outlined in Romans to contemporary evangelicalism, the sacraments, Catholic theology, pastoral and evangelistic ministry.

F.F. Bruce, *Paul: Apostle of the Free Spirit*, Paternoster, 1977
A readable account of Paul's life and work plus key issues.

David L. Edwards, with John Stott, *Essentials*, Hodder and Stoughton, 1988
A stimulating debate by two leading scholars defending somewhat different positions on a number of issues, in particular the nature and authority of the Bible and essential features of the gospel.

Matthew Fox, *Original Blessing*, Bear and Co., 1983
A controversial, challenging plea to right the balance, as the author sees it, by placing greater emphasis on the blessing of creation – God's earliest and most fundamental dealings with us, according to the author – rather than fall/redemption thinking.

V.P. Furnish, *Theology and Ethics in Paul*, Abingdon, 1968
By a careful, scholarly analysis of Paul's writings, the author seeks to demonstrate how ethical, not doctrinal considerations are at the root of Paul's writing.

J. Knox, *Life in Christ Jesus: Reflections on Romans 5 to 8*, SPCK, 1962
Valuable meditative material.

J. Koenig, *Charismata: God's Gifts for God's People*, Westminster, 1978
A comprehensive survey and assessment of the use of the charismatic gifts.

G.E. Ladd, *A Theology of the New Testament*, Lutterworth, 1974
A useful treatment of the teaching that God's judgment

has already taken place.

Leon Morris, *The Cross of Jesus,* Eerdmans, 1988
The author shows how Jesus' death on the cross answers such immediate problems as our sense of futility, loneliness, sickness and similar issues.

Alister McGrath, *Justification by Faith: What it means for us today,* Marshall Pickering, 1988
Provides a contemporary freshness and relevance to a teaching that, because of its association with Reformation controversy, has undeservedly appeared tiring and boring.

J. Murphy O'Connor, *Paul on Preaching,* Sheed and Ward, 1964
Covers both the theory and practice of Paul's preaching.

J. Reumann et al, *'Righteousness' in the New Testament,* Fortress, 1982
A scholarly dialogue between Catholics and Lutherans on the question of justification, a key teaching of Romans.

R.C. Sproul, *If there's a God, why are there atheists?,* Tyndale, 1988
Sproul shows that there are as many psychological and sociological explanations for unbelief as for belief. His penetrating analysis illuminates Paul's argument, in Romans 1, verses 18 and following, that we cannot plead ignorance.

J.K. Stendahl, *Paul amongst the Jews and Gentiles,* Fortress, 1976

A scholarly, detailed reinterpretation of our understanding of Paul, arguing that we read him in too introspective and individualistic a way.

J.V. Taylor, *The Go-between God*, SCM, 1972
A powerful and evocative treatment of the person and work of the Holy Spirit.

Stephen Travis, *Christ and the Judgment of God*, Marshall Pickering, 1986
A careful New Testament study of unpopular themes such as wrath, judgment and retribution.

S. Westerholm, *Israel's Law and the Church's Faith*, Eerdmans, 1988
A scholarly work defending a traditional understanding of Paul's thought on this subject and making a distinctive contribution to that understanding.

J.H. Yoder, *The Politics of Jesus*, Eerdmans, 1972
The author has an illuminating chapter on justification by grace through faith, which draws heavily on the first eight chapters of Romans.

Useful treatments of present-day faith and life issues raised in Romans

David Augsburger, *Caring enough to forgive*, Regal, 1981
A readable, appealing case is made out for the advantages of forgiveness and the work necessary to produce it.

Don Baker and Emery Nestor, *Depression*, Multnomah, 1983
A helpful personal account of depression by a sufferer and his counsellor.

Robert and Julia Banks, *The Church Comes Home: A new basis for community and mission*, Albatross, 1990
An account of the New Testament basis and the practical outworking of home churching in the experience of the authors and others.

Sheila Cassidy, *Sharing the Darkness*, Darton, Longman and Todd, 1988
A personal story by one who is confronting the problems of caring for the terminally ill.

Jacques Ellul, *The New Demons*, Mowbrays, 1975
Examines religiosity and effectively contrasts true and false religion.

Os Guiness, *Doubt: Faith in two minds*, Lion, 1976
Examines the role of doubt in the growth of faith.

Brian Hill, *The Greening of Christian Education*, Lancer, 1985
This book contains a helpful explanation of the relationship between belief and faith.

Robert Jewett, *Christian Tolerance; Paul's Message to the Modern Church*, Westminster, 1982
The writer argues that tolerance is central to Paul's teaching.

Merle R. Jordan, *Taking on the Gods: The task of the pastoral counsellor*, Abingdon, 1986
The author relates Paul's teaching on God's unconditional love to the role of the pastoral counsellor.

Alice and Stephen Lawhead, *Pilgrim's Guide to the New Age*, Lion, 1986
A conducted tour through the features of the so-called New Age, providing a link between modern philosophies and the world view of the book of Romans.

J.I. Packer, *Hot Tub Religion and other thoughts on Christian living in the material world*, Tyndale, 1988
Engages in metaphor to bring to life some cogent arguments against contemporary hedonism.

J.I. Packer, *Knowing God*, Hodder and Stoughton, 1973
In expanding our horizons on the character and work of God, the author places particular emphasis on Romans chapters 1 to 8.

J.I. Packer and Thomas Howard, *Christianity: The true humanism*, Word, 1985
Packer's clear-headed arguments combined with Howard's brilliant literary skills produce a scathing critique of secular humanism and present Christianity as the true humanism.

Lance Pierson, *No-Gay Areas: Pastoral Care of Homosexual Christians*, Grove, 1989
Deals sensitively with the pastoral care of homosexual

Christians, an area not covered by Paul when he deals with homosexuality in Romans chapter 1.

John Stott, *Christian Mission in the Modern World*, Falcon, 1977
A carefully argued biblical summary of the meaning of mission and evangelism.

Paul Tournier, *The Strong and the Weak*, SCM, 1963
The writer argues against classifying people into strong and weak. Rather, he sees God taking us as we are and working with us.

Notes

Notes

Notes

Notes

Notes

Notes

Notes